ENGLISH ✳ HERITAGE

Book of
Iron Age
Britain

ENGLISH ⊞ HERITAGE

Book of
Iron Age
Britain

Barry Cunliffe

B.T. Batsford Ltd/English Heritage
London

First published 1995
All rights reserved. No part of this publication
may be reproduced, in any form or by any means,
without permission from the Publisher

Typeset by Lasertext Ltd, Stretford,
Manchester M32 0JT
Printed and bound in Great Britain by
The Bath Press, Bath, Avon

Published by B.T. Batsford Ltd
4 Fitzhardinge Street, London W1H 0AH

A CIP catalogue record for this book is
available from the British Library

ISBN 0 7134 71840 (cased)
0 7134 72995 (limp)

Contents

Illustrations

Colour Plates

Acknowledgements

I would like to record my thanks to Peter Kemmis Betty and Stephen Johnson who invited me to write this book, thus bringing upon themselves the task of reading the first draft of the manuscript. Their helpful criticisms were gratefully received and acted upon, resulting in a text which is crisper and more jargon-free than it would otherwise have been.

In preparing the book I have benefited very considerably from the help of my colleagues at the Institute of Archaeology at Oxford: Lynda Smithson translated my increasingly illegible scribble into an immaculate typescript; Alison Wilkins prepared all the line drawings which are not otherwise credited; while Bob Wilkins and Jennie Lowe produced prints of photographs from the Institute's archives (**37**, **39**, **40**, **51**, **52**, **54**, **63**, **69**, **73**, **74**, **76**, **79**, **82**). Edward Impey, advised by Sonia Hawkes, drew the reconstruction of the Cow Down House (**21**): the other reconstructions were prepared by Chris Evans and Judith Dobie of English Heritage. Photographs were provided by Steve Hartgroves of the Cornish Archaeological Unit (**4**, **5**, **28**, **31**), the British Museum (**6**, **8**, **58**, **65**, **70**), the Museum of Archaeology and Ethnology at Cambridge (**87**, **88**), the Cambridge University Committee for Aerial Photography (**1**, **23**, **41**), Winchester Archaeological Unit (**80**), the National Museum of Scotland (**10**, **11**, **67**), the Museum of the Iron Age, Andover (**7**), Terry Manby (**9**) and Bill Marsden (**48**).

Preface

I was asked to write this book at the time when I was just completing the third edition of *Iron Age Communities in Britain*. My immediate reaction was to say no but after a while I found myself thinking more and more about the attraction of writing an interpretative essay, freed from the need to assemble and assess the huge quantity of data which formed the necessary basis of the textbook. The attraction soon became a compulsion: what follows is the result.

The format of this series imposes a welcome and creative constraint. In an essay of 40,000 words it is necessary to be highly selective and to rise above the disparate mass of evidence in order to discover the patterns and perspectives inherent, but often obscured, within it. From such a viewpoint it becomes increasingly obvious that the development of Britain cannot begin to be understood in isolation – the communities of these islands are, and always have been, part of a much broader European system. It is for this reason that, from time to time, we pause, in this book, to view the wider European scene.

Yet it would be quite wrong to imply that the development of British society was controlled from outside. Far from it. As we will see, the varied landscapes of these islands encouraged social diversity: they provided constraints to which communities responded with fascinating originality. The story of British society must always be structured around the framework of the land but often the catalyst for change is external.

The first millennium BC was a time of dramatic change in Europe, dominated by the emergence of Rome as a megastate. In Britain, on the very extremity of these developments, it was a time of huge social and economic change which saw the ending of the Neolithic and Bronze Age cycle and the beginning of a world which, in all its essentials, was to change little until the oceans were conquered in the sixteenth century.

Our theme then is of social change within an insular society sitting on the periphery of a world in revolution. It is an epic well worth the telling.

1

The land

It is a common misapprehension that because Britain is an island it was cut off from the Continent, its communities developing in grand isolation, only occasionally being jolted from their comfortable complacency by incoming bands of warriors prepared to brave the dangers of the Channel and the North Sea. Throughout prehistory the reality was, in all probability, very different. The concept of 'our island fortress' is a political construct of the modern world, born with the threat of the Armada and encouraged from time to time thereafter when Continentals like Napoleon and Hitler cast covetous eyes across the Channel. Nineteenth- and twentieth-century scholars could back-project this model, pointing to the invasions of the Normans, the Vikings, the Saxons and the Romans, and could conclude that thus it had always been. Such generalizations may be helpful at one level but at another they can be very misleading. The conquests and folk movements of the first millennium AD were characteristic of the phase of European history dominated by the rise and fall of the megastate of Rome. Before that, in the first and second millennia BC, the dynamics of European society were very different. This is not to say that there were no folk movements and aggressive onslaughts but simply that the scale was altogether in a different register.

Another preconception that we need to rid ourselves of at the outset is our modern sense of cognitive geography. We are used to seeing Britain neatly and accurately depicted on a map separated by sea from the Continent and with its major lines of communication focusing on London. The vision is one of inward-looking insularity and our experiences tend to reinforce this. Leaving Oxford early one morning and travelling by coach, aeroplane, hire car and boat I was able to explore the broch of Mousa on the Shetlands by late afternoon. On another occasion, again leaving Oxford, it took only an hour and a half to reach Portsmouth and then an interminable nine hours at sea before arriving at the coast of Brittany. Experiences of this kind condition our attitudes to geography. But the availability of maps and improved communications are a recent phenomenon. That there may be other visions of geography was vividly brought home to me in Orkney in the mid-1970s, when I was standing on the harbourside at Kirkwall talking to a local farmer about the autumn export of cattle. When asked where his cattle went he said that they were sent south. Pressed as to where, he said, 'far south . . . to Aberdeen, and sometimes much further – to the English plain beyond'. His cognitive geography was not one conditioned by maps and air travel but was informed by his own observations and conversations on the quayside.

Let us then put aside our modern preconceptions and think of the past. The vast bulk of the population of the English Midlands in the early Middle Ages are unlikely to have

1 *The rocky promontories of south-western Britain, here Treryn Dinas, St Levan, are closely comparable to those of Armorica and Galicia. These regions were bound together by complex networks of trade and exchange operating along the Atlantic sea routes.*

travelled more than 30–50km (20 or 30 miles) from their homes. For them their horizons were strictly limited and access to information restricted in the extreme. Yet a man of Winchelsea or Rye was in an entirely different position. He may not have ventured far but on the quays he would have heard talk of a wider world and in the taverns may well have drunk Gascon wine poured from elegant Saintonge pitchers. His vision of the world would have been different. For him, to travel to Oxford to visit the Benedictine House would have meant a far longer and more arduous journey than a visit to the Brothers' monastery at Fécamp. Much the same may well have been true in the first millennium BC when mobility by land is likely to have been even more restricted.

The most helpful way to visualize the all-important question of mobility and information exchange is to accept that, while the sea can link, the land can divide. Thus Britain might better be considered not as an entity but as a series of zones defined in terms of their degree of relationship to the Continent. Using this approach we can recognize three zones of contact. The most obvious is that linked by the Straits of Dover enabling the communities of south-east Britain, occupying the littoral

2 *The British Isles has always been closely linked to Continental Europe. The map summarizes the principal axes of contact in the first millennium BC.*

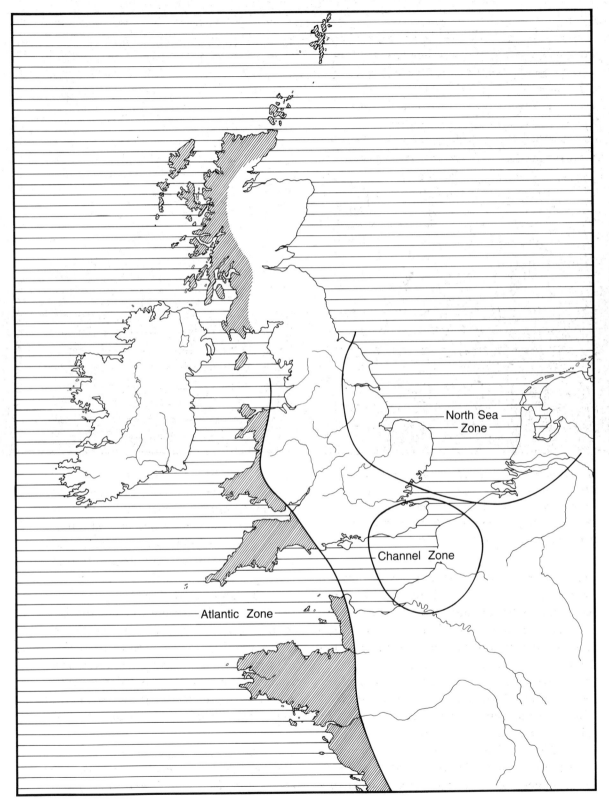

North Sea Zone

Channel Zone

Atlantic Zone

between Newhaven and North Foreland, to maintain easy contact with the French coast from Calais to Le Havre and by means of the Seine and the Somme to much of the French hinterland.

The southern extremity of the North Sea constitutes another zone of contact, putting the river systems of eastern England, from the Thames to the Yare, within easy reach of the rivers of the Low Countries. Distances are not great: the direct route between Holland and Norfolk is barely 170km (106 miles).

The west provides a more complex picture. Here peninsulas of old hard rock thrust into the Atlantic – Holyhead, St David's Head, Land's End, Finistère and Finisterre (1). They are all, to their inhabitants, the ends of the world but the seas between linked them, providing a web of ancient routes along which sailors could carry commodities and ideas, plying the coasts and seas they knew, and in the ports interacting with others of like mind familiar with the sea-ways beyond. This complex network of overlapping systems created a broad corridor of movement, at its extremes stretching between the ports of Andalucia and the Islands of Shetland. In the Iron Age a family living in Cornwall had more in common culturally with a community in Brittany than it did with one in East Anglia or for that matter Hampshire.

Taking this more outward-looking perspective it is possible therefore to view Britain not centrifugally but centripetally – not as an entity but as a series of outward-looking zones. The map (2) helps to visualize this but like all helpful generalizations it is grossly over-simple. What it does do, however, is to provide a focus which redresses the imbalance caused by accidents of modern research. Looking at the Ordnance Survey Map of Southern Britain in the Iron Age one might form the impression that Wessex was the centre. Our Fig. 3, on the contrary, might be thought to suggest that Wessex was in fact a periphery – an inbetween land bordering other more distinctive zones with wider horizons. That we should be forced

to reverse our perspectives occasionally is a healthy exercise and can sometimes lead to a better understanding.

Geographical determinism in archaeology is unfashionable and yet, looking at the landscape of Britain, one is forced to admit that the geomorphology of the island must have played a significant part in constraining the nature of settlement, thus influencing the social systems that could emerge. The issue was first given substance by Sir Cyril Fox in a brilliant introductory essay published as *The Personality of Britain* in 1932. Using the archaeological data then to hand Fox divided Britain into a highland and a lowland zone – it was essentially a north-west/south-east divide. While there is still much truth in this simple generalization the picture needs to be modified. A more appropriate division of the land is between east and west. The predominantly upland nature of the west, from Dartmoor to the Grampians, combined with the present weather systems means that the western part of the country has a high rainfall of over 250cm (100in.) per year while the eastern extremity of Eastern Anglia has under 150cm (60in.). Factors of this kind would have created constraints directly affecting the food-generating regimes and this in its turn is likely to have offered some limitation to the socio-economic systems which developed. Add to this other factors such as differences in the number of hours of sunshine each July day – crucial to the ripening of crops – and the point that Britain exhibits considerable extremes of microclimate will become immediately apparent. In other words, in the past, as now, the kind of agriculture that could be practised on, say, the downs of Kent would simply not have been possible in the Outer Hebrides. The point may be self-evident but it needs to be stressed to explain the most bewildering diversity in settlement and social systems apparent in the Iron Age, the more so then because the com-

3 Britain presents a varied landscape which has had a significant influence on settlement pattern.

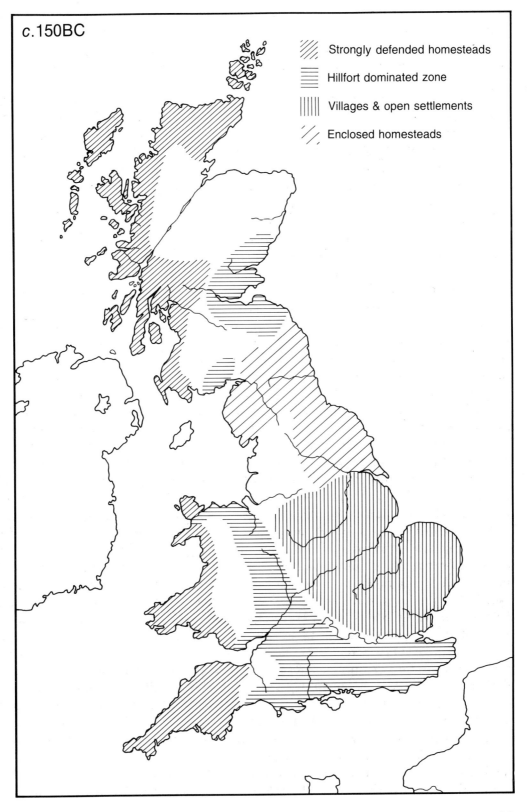

c.150BC

- ⧄ Strongly defended homesteads
- ☰ Hillfort dominated zone
- ⦀ Villages & open settlements
- ⁄ Enclosed homesteads

paratively simple technologies available did not allow communities to override geography.

The land of Britain, then, presented to the prehistoric inhabitants a mosaic of microregions each with its own constraints and opportunities. The dynamic relationship between the social group and its environment generated a cultural landscape of great variety, but standing back from the detail it is possible to generalize and to divide it into five broad zones: south-west, north-west, north-east, east and central south (**3**). It says much for the dominant role played by environment that even today this five-fold division is a useful generalization in attempting to understand social and economic differences.

4 *An abandoned Bronze Age settlement and its adjacent fields on Leskernick Hill, Altarnun, Cornwall.*

Against the immutable structure created, in the first instance, by solid geology must be seen the far more subtle patterns of change caused by climatic variation and by anthropomorphic factors – the interference of man in his environment. These are difficult matters to untangle. A widely accepted view is that the first quarter of the first millennium BC saw a dramatic fall of 2°C in overall mean temperature. There was a slight improvement about the middle of the millennium and a return to colder conditions towards the end. Such a fluctuation sounds unimpressive but in reality it could have shortened the growing season by up to five weeks. For upland communities in the north, where summer sunshine was crucial for ripening the crop, such a fluctuation would have been disastrous. It is dramatically reflected in the

swathes of abandoned landscapes, dating to the second and early first millennia BC, found in certain upland areas of northern and western Britain where communities were forced by changing climates to abandon traditional farmlands for the more congenial climates of lower altitudes (**4**). Such changes, even if spread over several centuries, are likely to have caused social disruption.

In parallel with these temperature variations there were also considerable changes in rainfall. From the late second millennium BC until about 700 BC the climate became noticeably wetter but after the middle of the millennium there was a return to drier conditions. In the west and in the highlands generally, where precipitation

5 *Landscape continuity at Zennor, Cornwall. A courtyard-house settlement of the early first millennium AD lies abandoned but the boundaries of many of its fields have influenced the more recent landscape. (See also* **colour plate 6**.*)*

was greatest, the effects of these changes would have been intensified. On Dartmoor it is possible to show that over this period the higher reaches developed thicker and more extensive peat bogs which drove settlement from the uplands. The recurring nature of this problem is nicely demonstrated by the brief colonization of these same regions in the early Middle Ages and the rapid abandonment again as the worsening climate of the fourteenth century took its toll. The environment on the fringes of settlement was fickle and in the abandoned farms of the early first millennium BC and early second millennium AD we witness the pioneering efforts of early inhabitants beaten back by nature.

Man's ability to initiate irreversible changes in his own environment is well known. Deforestation and the extension of ploughed land is likely, over the broad sweep of the prehistoric period, to have wrought considerable change and as population increased and more land was brought under the plough so the rate of change would have accelerated. Work in the river valleys of the English Midlands shows that alluviation took place on a massive scale in the first millennium BC, completely changing the productive potential of huge tracts of land. Factors of this kind, together with the depletion of soil nutrients as the result of intensified cropping, cannot have failed to have had an effect on the way communities utilized their environment. In short, throughout the period which concerns us, the landscape of Britain was constantly changing. In some areas and at some times rate of change was rapid – for the local communities perhaps even catastrophic – elsewhere change would have been imperceptible. But that environmental change was a constant reality is a fact we must not forget.

To take stock – we have briefly explored three facets of the stage upon which the communities of Iron Age Britain were constrained to act out their lives: the local regions and their ease of access to the Continent; the structure of the land; and the subtle changes to which the environment was continuously subjected. The situation, then, was an infinitely subtle interplay between immutability and the restless dynamics of change.

Some communities, because of their relative isolation and comparatively static environment, changed little over considerable periods of time (5). Others occupying territories on or close to corridors of communication were open to external influences. Yet others, under pressure from their changing environments, were forced to evolve or die. Thus, there were conserving societies and innovating societies. The rate of change varied from area to area and from time to time but as a generalization we may say that for the most part the communities of the west experienced far less social change in the Iron Age than did those of the south-east. In Cornwall, for example, the basic settlement enclosure – the round – showed little change between the late second millennium BC and the late first millennium AD, whereas in the south-east an urban system had evolved, matured and all but disappeared during that span. The reason for this stark difference is that the two zones belonged to different inter-regional systems. The south-east, by virtue of its geographical proximity to the Continental heartlands, shared in the innovative forces which gripped the region, facilitated in part by ease of communication and an overall agrarian fertility, while the west was part of a totally different regional system – the Atlantic zone – with its rugged face to the ocean: it was a kaleidoscope of small self-contained communities – an outward-looking periphery.

That today the same divide persists is a dramatic reaffirmation of a basic geographical truth. The fellow feeling of the, so-called, 'Celtic west' which brings Galician bagpipes regularly to perform in Breton *festivals folkloriques* and makes economic sense of a regular ferry link between Cork and Roscoff, contrasts with the golden economic crescent stretching from the English Midlands across northern France and Germany to the Po valley. These are modern reflections of the power of the interacting forces which were already shaping Britain three millennia ago.

2

The people: race, language and population

Of these complex issues what can we possibly hope to know? The Roman historian, Tacitus, writing at the end of the first century AD, took something of a minimalist view. 'Who the first inhabitants of Britain were,' he wrote, 'whether natives or immigrants remains obscure; one must remember we are dealing with barbarians'

6 *An attempt to visualize an Iron Age Briton. Reconstruction based on the well preserved body found in the bog at Lindow (see 8).*

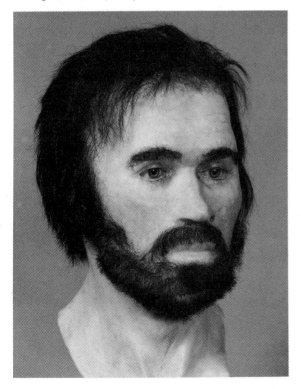

(Tacitus, *Agricola* II). With that it is difficult to argue. Yet even the circumspect Tacitus cannot resist adding a few observations and speculations. The Britons' physical characteristics vary, he notes, a variation which is suggestive. 'The reddish hair and large limbs of the Caledonians [in Scotland] proclaim their Germanic origins, the swarthy faces of the Silures [in south-east Wales], the tendency of their hair to curl, and the fact that Spain lies opposite, all lead one to believe that Spaniards crossed in ancient times . . . . The peoples nearest to the Gauls likewise resemble them . . . it seems likely that the Gauls settled in the island lying so close to their shores.' That there were physical differences between populations we can reasonably accept but Tacitus's explanations are of course no more than speculation (**6**, **7**, **8**, **colour plate 12**).

Another writer to take a passing interest in these matters was Julius Caesar who had the advantage of actually confronting Britons in their own country during his campaigns in 55 and 54 BC. In offering a brief background to his readers Caesar says of the Britons, 'The interior . . . is inhabited by people who claim, on the strength of their own traditions, to be indigenous. The coastal areas are inhabited by invaders who crossed from Belgium for the sake of plunder and then, when the fighting was over, settled there and began to work the land' (Caesar, *De Bello Gallico* V,12). He goes on to add that the population, presumably of the

7 *A modern vision of an Iron Age warrior chief stands guard at the Museum of the Iron Age, Andover.*

south-east with which he was familiar, was extremely large.

Invasions and the Celtic language

The opinions of Caesar and of Tacitus provided the foundations upon which the theories of nineteenth- and twentieth-century commentators were constructed. This is not the place to re-examine, in any detail, the development of archaeological thought on the subject but a brief comment must be offered if only because some of the theories developed last century and in the early years of this, while the discipline was in its infancy, are still occasionally, almost a century on, being stated as facts. The basic model adopted to explain the peopling of Britain was one of successive invasions from the Continent. It was a model consistent with the examples of recent history and one which could be claimed to have been given support by Caesar's statements about settlers from Belgium.

In 1890 Arthur Evans attempted to give some physical reality to these Belgian settlers by suggesting that a group of burials found at Aylesford in Kent could be ascribed to them. Further elaboration of the invasionist model came in the decade between 1912 and 1922 in theories developed by J. Abercromby, O.G.S. Crawford and H. Peake. It was Peake's view that Britain received three distinct waves of invaders before the Belgae. The first in 1200 BC and the second in 900 BC were Goidelic Celts while the third about 300 BC were a group of Brythonic Celts. This model sought to link changes observed in material culture, represented in the archaeological record, to contemporary linguistic theories.

Linguists had characterized surviving Celtic languages into two groups, Goidelic which included Irish, Manx and Scots Gaelic, and

8 *Lindow Man, found preserved in a Cheshire bog.*

Brythonic to which Welsh, Breton and Cornish belonged. The principal difference lay in the way in which the Indo-European QU was sounded. In Goidelic it remained a gutteral sound *qu* but in Brythonic it had been labialized to *p*. This difference is sometimes characterized as Q-Celtic and P-Celtic. Given the assumed antiquity of Q-Celtic and its distribution around the western extremity of the Celtic-speaking world it is easy to see how the theory developed that Q-Celtic spread first everywhere, reaching the Atlantic seaboard, and that the more 'evolved' P-Celtic was brought in later, replacing the archaic Q-Celtic in Armorica, Cornwall, Wales and England, where a substratum of Brythonic place names could be found beneath those derived from the Latin, Germanic and Norman French spoken by later invaders. The theory had the advantage of being contained and elegantly simple, and the successive incomings which it implied could be linked to virtually any archaeological assemblage that was considered to be sufficiently 'foreign' in appearance to allow it to be assigned to an invading group.

Much has, of course, been written on the subject in the last 70 years. The invasionist theory remained popular until the 1960s when it began to be challenged and fell from favour. Meanwhile the researches of linguists have shown just how complex and uncertain the early development of language can be. Later displacements of population could also have complicated the picture with Goidelic Celtic being carried to Scotland from Northern Ireland in the mid-first millennium AD and Brythonic being imposed on Armorica by settlers coming from south-west Britain at the same time.

The old theories, which linked archaeological 'evidence' of invasion to the introduction of language groups, are an example of circularity in argument. As archaeologists abandoned invasionist theories, so linguists began to reassess their evidence. The general position now, widely held by many scholars in the field, is that the Indo-European language was introduced into Britain perhaps as early as the early Neolithic period and it was from this common base in Britain and much of western Europe that the Celtic language developed. The differences between Q-Celtic and P-Celtic would then be seen as the result of divergent development between different indigenous groups, owing little to successive waves of invaders. In other words, dialects of Celtic were to be heard over much of western Europe, as far west as the Atlantic fringes, long before the beginning of the first millennium BC. The differences between the Goidelic of Ireland and the Isle of Man and the Brythonic of Britain and probably Gaul would therefore most likely be the result of the relative isolation of the western islands in contrast to the contacts maintained by Britain and Gaul.

Tacitus, writing of the area of Britain close to Gaul, records that there was no great difference in language on the two sides of the Channel but goes on to tell us that the Britons of the south-east were eager, after the Roman invasion, to learn Latin. Even so it is clear from place-name evidence, and from names recorded on lead tablets found in the sacred spring at Bath, that Celtic names persisted throughout the Roman occupation. In the west and north, in Cornwall, Wales, Ireland and Scotland, away from the heavy hand of Romanization and of the later Germanic incursions, the living language survived.

If, then, we can uncouple the language of Celtic from distinctive assemblages of archaeological material and concepts of folk movement, how 'Celtic' was Britain in the sense that it shared in what some writers have characterized as a pan-European Celtic culture, spread largely by folk movements arising in north-eastern France and southern Germany in the fifth century BC?

That there were massive migrations of people, called 'Celts' or 'Gauls' by broadly contemporary classical writers, in Europe during the second half of the first millennium there

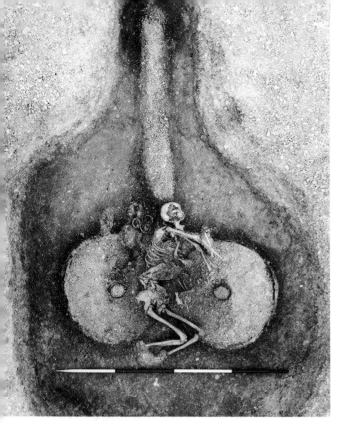

9 *A vehicle burial found at Wetwang Slack, Yorkshire. Burials of this kind were once thought to have been introduced into Britain by invasion from Continental Europe (see also* **34***).*

can be no reasonable doubt. Huge populations, spreading through the Alps, settled in the Po valley and from there raided Italy, devastating Rome in 390 BC; others migrated into Transdanubia, some thrusting eastwards into Transylvania in the protection of the Carpathians while others marauded through the Balkans. In 279 a substantial horde was besieging the sanctuary of Apollo at Delphi, while a few decades later their descendants were causing havoc among the Hellenistic cities of the Aegean coast of Asia Minor. The monumentalizing of their defeat by the kings of Pergamon gave rise to some of the finest statuary of the Hellenistic world, of which the famous 'Dying Gaul' is a later Roman copy. It was their descendants, now settled peaceably in central Anatolia, who received the crisp rebuke from St Paul recorded in his famous Letter to the Galatians (the same word as Gaul). The restless migrations of these

Celts or Gauls were still continuing in the middle of the first century BC when Caesar decided to deflect the movement of a whole tribe living in Switzerland, the Helvetii, from their planned migration to the west coast of France some 600km (375 miles) away.

The question for us is did these massive disruptions impinge at all on the British Isles? It used to be thought that they did. Weapons, hillforts and pottery styles in the south were paraded in support of an invasion from the area of the Marne, while chariot burials in Yorkshire, closely comparable to those found in northern France and Belgium, were seen as clear evidence of a warrior incursion using the Humber as a point of entry (**9**). Today few would support the idea of a Marnian invasion and doubts have been expressed about the precise interpretation of the Yorkshire burials, some writers arguing that they could more reasonably be explained as the emulation of an exotic burial tradition by a local elite. Yet even if this is so, it implies a degree of contact – ideas could not at that time cross seas without the intermediary of people.

As with so much of archaeology, interpretation in the end rests with the individual observer and observers are susceptible to fashion. On balance I would argue that there is no evidence in the British Isles to suggest that a population group of any size migrated from the Continent during the first millennium BC, always remembering, however, the wise platitude that absence of evidence is not evidence of absence. I have in mind here the salutary warning of a distribution map showing the occurrence of 'Celtic' finds in Greece and the Aegean. Only three or four small items are known, yet in 279 BC 40,000 Celtic warriors caused havoc as far south as the Gulf of Patras over a period of many months. They remain, however, archaeologically invisible.

If the current, widely held, view is correct, that Britain escaped the impact of folk movement from the Continent in the first millennium BC (though for the Belgae see below, p. 63), it remains to explain the nature of the similarities seen between the material assemblages of the British Isles and those of Continental Europe.

Contacts between Britain and the Continent

It is clear from a wide variety of evidence that the British Isles was in close contact with Continental Europe throughout the first millennium BC. The most self-evident contacts are displayed by items of prestige military equipment. Throughout the latter part of the Bronze Age exchange networks brought to Britain a variety of weapon types, particularly swords, developed by Continental craftsmen. These were copied, and often improved upon, by British metalworkers. This same pattern continued throughout the Iron Age without a break – though the volume of imports, reflecting the intensity of contact, seems to have fluctuated. In the seventh century came the long Hallstatt slashing swords of bronze and sometimes of iron. The sixth and fifth centuries saw later Hallstatt antennae-hilted swords and daggers and the first daggers and swords of the La Tène period – artefacts associated on the Continent with bands of migrating 'Celts'. Thereafter the curvilinear art styles of the La Tène period were eagerly adopted and adapted in Britain for a wide range of embellishments, from the sword sheaths and shields of the elite to comparatively humble pottery. The overall impression given by this range of material is that Britain and Europe were part of a common market within which materials and ideas spread freely.

But the common market analogy is not strictly correct. A 'market economy' had not by this stage developed. The movement of commodities was carefully regulated within the constraints of elite-dominated exchange systems. Items passed as gifts, both horizontally between equals in the upper échelons of the social hierarchy and vertically downwards between paramounts and their dependants, in cycles of gift exchange. This kind of system is known as an embedded economy.

If we look at the range of imported items, or concepts of items, in the seventh century (the Hallstatt period) we can see that they fall neatly into two broad groups: warrior equipment and personal trinkets. The warrior equipment consists of the long slashing sword and its sheath and the horse decked out with an array of bronze-ornamented tack. The personal items include razors, toilet sets, brooches, pins and bracelets. The warrior equipment would have been suitable as gifts between men of high rank, while the other items are the sorts of things that could have been passed down the social hierarchy. The simplest model to explain these scatters of material in Britain is to see them as the result of the adoption of similar ideas and patterns of behaviour across Britain and the Continent, which would make gifts of this kind acceptable over large tracts of territory. Thirty years ago it was conventional to interpret Hallstatt metalwork in Britain as an indication of invaders – mounted warriors from France and Germany crossing the North Sea to establish new domains for themselves. Today there is a distinct preference to see the pattern as reflecting diplomatic gifts of armour and horses between elites. There can be no doubt that men and equipment moved across the sea but most likely it was in a context of diplomacy rather than naked aggression.

The flow of goods was not always one way. That British swords and daggers are occasionally found on the Continent is an indication of some kind of reciprocity. What other commodities may have been carried back to the courts of the Continental elite is uncertain – they are archaeologically invisible – but possibilities include woollen fabrics and garments, metals and even hunting dogs, for all of which Britain, later, was justly famed.

It is in this context of elite emulation that it may be possible to interpret the chariot burials of Yorkshire mentioned above (9). While it is possible that the tradition was introduced by a group of 'invaders', it is equally possible that this exotic burial ritual was adopted by the

10 *Engraved drinking horn terminals from Torrs, Kircudbrightshire, Scotland, are among the masterpieces of 'Celtic art' made by British craftsmen conversant with Continental tradition.*

western sea-ways remained consistently high, the motivation presumably being trade in metals of which tin, by virtue of its rarity, was particularly important.

By these complex networks of contact the inhabitants of the British Isles were able to share in the cultural developments of Europe. The brilliant metalworkers' art of the La Tène period – Celtic Art as it is more widely known – spread rapidly to Britain and local schools of great vitality emerged eventually to create their own distinctive insular interpretations (**10, 11**). In short the Celtic-speaking inhabitants of Britain would probably have been able to communicate fairly easily with most of the communities of central and western Europe: they shared many of the same social conventions, beliefs and values and enjoyed the same vigorous art. The mobility of people and of information created a remarkable, if superficial, degree of similarity over vast tracts of territory.

Population growth

If one were to compare the evidence for settlement in say 1000 BC with that for 100 BC the

11 *The pony cap from Torrs brilliantly decorated, in native 'Celtic' style, with a repoussé rendering of a bird.*

local elite simply to distinguish themselves from the lower ranks by stressing their cosmopolitan aspirations. A more recent parallel would be the adoption of the tea-drinking ritual, with all the paraphernalia of teapots and teacups, by the English upper classes in the eighteenth century: [no-one would interpret this as a Chinese invasion of Britain.]

Sufficient will have been said to suggest that Britain remained in active contact with the Continent and the sea-ways must have seen a constant flow of people and goods. The volume of exchange is difficult to quantify with any precision but it seems to have been considerable until the fifth century, after which contacts seem to have diminished until the beginning of the first century BC, when a considerable intensification in trade was initiated by new demands emanating from the Mediterranean world. As a generalization this has a degree of reality but when looked at in detail a more complex picture emerges, which suggests that throughout the period movement along the

24

overriding impression given would be that the population had dramatically increased during the course of the first millennium, yet it is very difficult to give even approximate figures. A variety of estimates have, however, been offered for the population of Britain, during the high point of the second century AD, varying from 3–6 million. These figures are at best little more than informed guesses but they indicate an order of magnitude. If we assume a gradual, but not necessarily even, rise in population over the first millennium, then we might be dealing with a population beginning at less than a million in the Late Bronze Age and rising to three or four times that number by the end of

12 *The Islands of Shetland, with their finely preserved Iron Age settlements, allow the density of settlement to be appreciated. The shaded areas represent their supposed territories.*

the millennium. But let us stress these are guesses not estimates.

Population was by no means evenly distributed across the country. In areas of Hampshire, Northamptonshire and Gloucestershire, where detailed surveys have been undertaken, it looks very much as though by the third or second century BC these favoured landscapes were very densely settled. But such densities have not been evenly recorded across the whole country. In Shetland for instance, where the well-built nature of the settlements ensures their recognition today, it has been argued convincingly that the available land was by no means totally colonized (**12, colour plate 1**). In other areas like the Weald, the Forest of Dean and the New Forest, as well as the uplands of the west and north, settlement appears, at least on present evidence, to have been sparse. All this is only to be expected – the population is likely to have been concentrated on the lighter and more easily worked soils of the chalk and limestone hills and the river valleys. Infertile sand and heavily wooded clay were generally avoided, though in some areas of Northamptonshire there is clear evidence that the clayland was being colonized by the third and second centuries – which might suggest pressure on land.

What emerges, then, is a varied pattern of settlement. Some areas were densely settled while between were empty tracts of heathland or forest. In favoured areas of the south-east, by the first century BC, it is likely that the population had grown to such an extent that stress had begun to develop as it always does when the size of the community begins to approach the holding capacity of the environment. When Caesar landed in Kent in 54 BC he was impressed by the number of settlements he encountered, describing the population as 'extremely large', large, that is, presumably by comparison with the Gaul he knew so well. The communities he encountered were evidently in a state of some tension one with another – which may, indeed, have been exacerbated by increasing settlement density.

Population dynamics are notoriously difficult to assess from the archaeological record but demographic factors are of considerable importance in attempting to understand the progress of social development. While we may never be able to be precise about the size of the population of Iron Age Britain we should at least be aware that it is a variable in the equation that cannot be ignored.

3

The great transition:
taming the land

In conventional terms the Bronze Age gave place to the Iron Age in Britain around 700 BC but this simple change in technological dependence, replacing one metal for another as the prime material for making weapons and tools, was of comparatively little significance when compared with the massive social and economic changes which were already well underway by this time. The great upheaval is as complex as it is fascinating and only in the last decade or two has it been possible to begin to disentangle some of the main threads.

Given the great diversity of the British Isles, generalization is difficult but to help order the evidence we can divide the period of change into two broad phases, 1100–800 BC and 800–400 BC: to understand the second, which is the substance of this chapter, it is necessary to say something of the earlier stages.

The prelude to change 1400–1100 BC

Some time around 1400–1300 BC there is evidence from some parts of the British Isles to suggest that societies were beginning to develop a more consistent attitude to the use of land: settlements were being established at fixed points and maintained over a considerable period of time and the landscape was being divided up by boundaries, the sheer magnitude of which suggests a degree of social organization which must have involved the agreement and participation of substantial groups working together. There is nothing surprising about

this – after all the great monuments of Silbury Hill and the henges built 1500 years or so before show that society was well able to cohere under coercive leadership to create communal works. What is different about the social organization of the landscape in the period c. 1400–1300 is that the community's effort was now being expended not on ritual structures, around which communities could focus, but upon the organization of the landscape to grow more and better crops and to minimise social conflict. We will return to possible explanations for this later (pp. 39).

These early organized landscapes have survived later changes only rarely. One of the most remarkable occurs around the fringes of Dartmoor where it owes its survival to the climatic deterioration we have noted above, which rendered these upland areas difficult to cultivate. Here huge systems of land division have been distinguished based on 'reaves' – drystone walls which may have served as the bases for hedges. In some cases where excavation has taken place, the more permanent stone phase was found to be preceded by a phase of timber fencing. The basis of the setting out was a long terminal reave, which usually marked the boundary between upland pasture and the more heavily utilized land. A series of parallel reaves sprang from it at right angles dividing the land into long strips. The areas of land parcelled up in this way were enormous. Units of between 200 and 600ha (500 and 1500

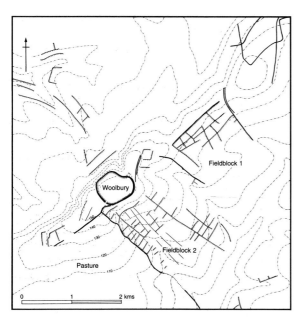

Fieldblock 1

Woolbury

Fieldblock 2

Pasture

0   1   2 kms

13 *At Woolbury, Hampshire, two blocks of coaxial fields were laid out in the mid Bronze Age as part of a systematic, and large-scale, scheme of land division. The hillfort was built centuries later but the fields continued in use.*

acres) were quite common and one system, at Rippon Tor, may have exceeded 4,500ha (11,250 acres). Associated with them were enclosures with circular huts and sometimes just scattered huts.

Today the Dartmoor reaves stand out as a remarkable example of land division but this is more because of their survival rather than their uniqueness. Similar land boundaries have been found on the Moors and Tabular Hills of Yorkshire and on Bodmin Moor, while in lowland areas, more heavily 'damaged' by subsequent land use, fragmentary indications of organized landscape have been found. At Fengate, on the fen edge near Peterborough, extensive systems of fields and enclosures defined by ditches have been revealed, and on the chalk downs of Wessex many remnants of coaxial fields – that is field systems laid out on a grid – can still be distinguished.

A good example of a typical Wessex field system survives on the east side of the Test valley in the vicinity of the later hillfort at Woolbury (**13**). Here blocks of land about 800m (2500ft) across were laid out on a south-east facing slope, based on a ditched boundary which ran along the hill crest. Each of the major land units was defined by boundary ditches between which there were regular systems of fields. The Woolbury system is particularly interesting in that it is possible to trace one boundary, still surviving remarkably intact, separating arable land from a tract of pasture which has never been ploughed and remains as common land even today. Similar tracts of coaxial fields can be traced east of the hillfort of Danebury and west of the hillfort of Quarley. While the proximity of early field systems and the much later hillforts may be coincidental, it is tempting to believe that the juxtaposition might represent some element of social continuity.

If these fragments of evidence from Yorkshire, East Anglia, Hampshire and Devon can be taken as a fair reflection of what was going on in southern Britain at the time, then we must conclude that the second half of the second millennium BC saw a remarkable change in the face of the countryside with an order and regularity being imposed upon it of a kind never before seen.

Between and among the chequer-board of fields were the settlements usually representing isolated communities of family or extended-family size. Where evidence survives it would seem that these farms remained in the same general location for generations, the various phases of rebuilding sometimes giving rise to a confused pattern of settlement structures.

What kind of social organization prevailed it is more difficult to say. There must have been considerable variety from one part of the country to another. The community living in the stone-built cellular houses at Jarlshof, on Shetland, may well have been similar in size and status to that occupying wooden houses on the Sussex Downs at Itford, but this does not mean that the complexity of the larger social group to which they belonged was the same.

The different soil conditions and different climates are likely to have conditioned, in part at least, the development of the social systems of which these family units were components.

In central southern Britain some hint of the broader social organization is provided by ditched enclosures located on prominent hilltops: places like Rams Hill on the Berkshire Downs, Harrow Hill in Sussex and Norton Fitzwarren in Somerset. Their size and location distinguish them from farmsteads and it has been suggested that they served as central places where the elements of the larger social group could interact – perhaps in periodic religious festivals associated with feasting and exchange.

14 *Strongly defended circular enclosures of the ninth and eighth centuries* BC *may be regarded as 'aristocratic' settlements. They concentrate in eastern Britain.*

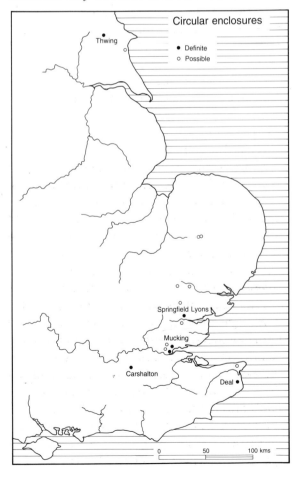

That exchanges did take place is amply demonstrated by the distribution of bronze tools and weapons. Judging by the different patterns, simpler items of lower prestige like tools were made and distributed over limited territories, while prestige items like swords tended to be made in fewer places and were dispersed more widely. These different patterns show that society must have been organized at a complex level.

To identify the elite at this time is not easy, largely because the prevailing burial rite – cremation and burial in urnfields – offers little chance of differentiating between the social status of individuals. We have, therefore, to rely largely on evidence derived from the excavation of settlements.

Eastern England 1100–800 BC

In recent years excavations in the east of England have revealed a distinctive type of settlement, usually a circular ditched enclosure (sometimes with two concentric ditches)

15 *A selection of the fully excavated Late Bronze Age circular enclosures of eastern Britain.*

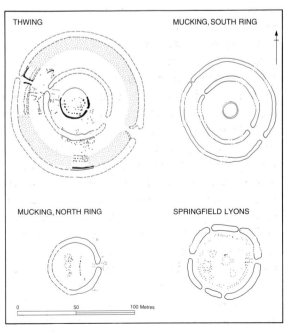

between 50 and 100m (165–330ft) in diameter containing one or more large, centrally-placed timber house. Examples of this kind of site have been excavated at Thwing in Yorkshire and at Mucking and Springfield Lyons in Essex (**14, 15**). South of the Thames there are less fully explored examples at Carshalton and Deal. Radiocarbon dates place these sites broadly within the bracket 1100–800 BC. The massiveness of the structures and the range of metalwork associated with them strongly suggest that they may have been the residences of the local elite, though other explanations – as communal/religious sites – are quite possible. The predominantly eastern distribution suggests that this is a regional phenomenon.

The Welsh Borderland 1100–800 BC

The Welsh Borderland provides a contrasting picture. Here, focused around the upper tributaries of the River Severn, a number of excavations on the sites of hillforts have produced evidence of hilltop enclosures, sometimes of very considerable size, dating to the period *c.* 1100–800 BC. At The Breiddin a timber-reinforced earth and stone bank enclosed an area of 30ha (75 acres) while barely 20km (32 miles) away the hilltop of Llwyn Bryn-dinas – only some 3.2ha (8 acres) – was defended by a dump rampart with a vertical stave fence. Other nearby enclosures include a palisade and early box rampart at Old Oswestry and possibly a double palisade at Ffridd Faldwyn. The variety of the enclosure boundaries and the disparity in size suggest that we are dealing with a complex pattern of development spanning several hundred years and no doubt reflecting different social functions. However the very size of these undertakings implies a vigorous and fast-evolving society whose strength and power may well have lain in their ability to extract and distribute the ample supplies of local copper.

Central southern Britain 1100–800 BC

Towards the end of this first stage of the period of transformation there is evidence that substantial hilltop enclosures were being constructed in central southern Britain (**16**). That so few have been examined by excavation, and few radiocarbon dates have been obtained, leaves a considerable area of uncertainty about their exact chronology and function. All are large, mostly falling between 10 and 30ha (25 and 75 acres), and in all cases the boundary 'defences' are comparatively slight. At Bathampton Hill, near Bath, the rampart was stone-faced, at Balksbury, near Andover, it was of dumped soil, while at Harting Beacon on the South Downs near Petersfield it was retained between two rows of upright timbers. Where excavations have taken place inside, very little evidence of occupation has been found but consistently settings of four posts have come to light. These structures are usually interpreted as 'granaries' in the archaeological literature but those found in the early hilltop enclosures are usually small, slight structures more appropriate for use as fodder ricks.

Exactly how to interpret these sites is difficult. That they are 'communal' structures is evident from the considerable expenditure of energy which would have been necessary to construct them but the apparent absence of significant occupation and the presence of possible fodder ricks might suggest that the enclosures performed some kind of pastoral function. Maybe they were the places to which the flocks and herds were driven at certain times of year when it was necessary to control them more closely for purposes of redistribution, culling or castration (not unlike the round-up of New Forest ponies today). The somewhat remote upland areas where these enclosures were often built would tend to support such an interpretation. A primary pastoral function of this kind does not, of course, exclude more complex social functions. In many European peasant societies seasonal round-ups were the occasion for social gatherings, for exchanges (of commodities and brides), for competitions and for religious observances. The fairs still held in Britain today, often on saints' days, are simply a modern

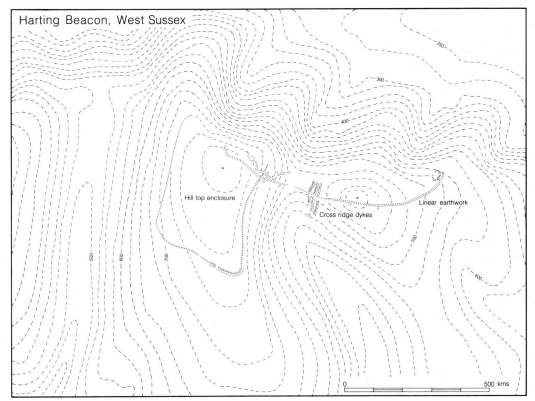

Harting Beacon, West Sussex

Hill top enclosure

Cross ridge dykes

Linear earthwork

0   500 kms

16 *The hilltop enclosure of Harting Beacon, West Sussex, is sited high on the South Downs and closely associated with linear earthworks. It is well located to provide corral space for substantial flocks and herds. The only features found inside were small four-post 'granaries' or, more likely, fodder racks.*

manifestation of the medieval fair which may well have been not so far removed from the activities which went on in the hilltop enclosures two thousand years earlier.

The four areas we have considered, the south-west, the east of England, the Welsh Borderland and central southern Britain seem to reflect rather different socio-economic systems but in each there is clear evidence of social complexity and of hierarchy. Other more remote areas like the Western Isles and the Orkneys and Shetlands probably developed simpler systems, dictated in part by the environmental niches in which the communities existed. The pattern

must have been infinitely more varied than our very partial picture allows us to distinguish.

Britain and Europe 800–550 BC

The eighth century BC was, for much of Britain, a time of rapid change. At a general level this can be seen in the range of bronze items in circulation. Throughout the early part of the first millennium a well-defined array of British-made weapons and tools, known in the south as the Wilburton complex and in the north as the Wallington complex and Poldar phase, were found quite widely. Some imported French types show that the south was in contact with the adjacent Continent. The eighth century saw a significant development. New weapon types emerge, typified by the long slashing sword named after the type site of Ewart Park, and a much wider range of European-inspired forms appear. In the south this includes distinctive material belonging to the 'Carp's-tongue sword complex', the distribution of which shows that southern Britain was now part of an Atlantic

31

province of trade and exchange stretching as far south as the Straits of Gibraltar and north to the Irish Sea. It may have been along this route that the fashion for circular bronze shields spread.

The reasons for the invigoration of the Atlantic route at this time are complex but one factor which is likely to have been of some significance is the dramatic development of the Phoenician trading entrepôt at Cadiz after about 800 BC, as a response to the demand for metals in the east Mediterranean and beyond. Cadiz was admirably sited to exploit the metals of the Iberian pyrite zone (silver, gold and tin) but it was also well placed to tap into traditional Atlantic routes along which copper, tin and the alloy bronze were regularly transported. The eighth century development of Cadiz and the intensification of Atlantic trade are too much of a coincidence to be unrelated.

At about this time there is also evidence for heightened trade across the North Sea, bringing to Britain a range of exotic material including horse gear. The contacts were maintained and even intensified during the seventh century. Horse gear (and horses?) continued to arrive in Britain together with buckets and swords of Hallstatt C type, all to be copied, and often improved upon, by native craftsmen.

As a broad generalization then we can say that the period c. 800–550 saw the British Isles, particularly the south and east, as part of a western European zone bound tightly by a web of closely interlocking exchange systems.

The middle of the sixth century saw new configurations developing in Europe. Phoenician power in Andalucia dramatically diminished, while at the same time, or a little after, the Hallstatt chiefdoms of western Europe began to develop trading contacts with the Mediterranean states at the expense of their western neighbours. The overall result of all this was that after the middle of the sixth century Britain's links with Europe declined quite noticeably, at least in volume.

The intensification and falling away of Continental contact during the period 800–550 BC coincides, as might be expected, with a range of social and economic changes which can be discerned among certain of the British communities. No doubt the two were causally linked but other factors of a more local kind, such as the effects of climatic deterioration and the momentum of change already underway, are likely to have contributed.

In the upland areas of the north and the west this was the time when greater precipitation would have tipped the ecological balance to such an extent that traditional farming regimes became impossible and many communities would have found it necessary to migrate to lower altitudes. This cannot have failed to have caused social disruption but it would be wrong to over-estimate the effects nationally. Stress is likely to have been localized and over much of southern and eastern Britain the changes may have passed unnoticed.

In eastern areas of Britain the collapse of the trade in bronze, which saw huge quantities of the alloy taken from circulation and buried in the ground or thrown into rivers and marshes presumably as votive offerings, coincides with the disappearance of the elite settlements defended by their circular enclosure ditches: none are known to date to after about 600 BC. While this may simply be a coincidence, it is tempting to suggest that the two factors are in some way linked. One possible explanation would be that the individuals of high status maintained their position only by controlling the supply and exchange of copper alloy goods. Over-stimulation of bronze production by demands emanating ultimately from the Mediterranean states, followed by reorientation within the heart of Europe, created surpluses in the west. The great increase in 'hoards' at this time could be explained as a socio-religious mechanism to remove surplus from circulation, thus increasing its value. That the elite settlements disappeared from the archaeological record might indicate that the system failed.

I have stressed that this is *one possible* expla-

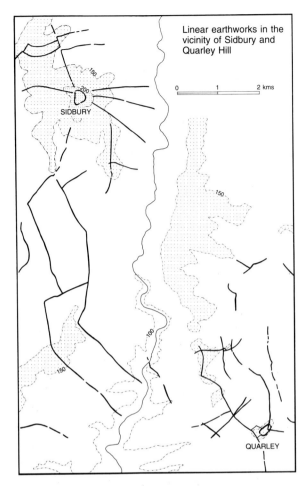

17 *Linear boundaries in east Wiltshire and west Hampshire on either side of the Bourne valley. The hillforts of Sidbury and Quarley were built later.*

18 *Aerial view of the Iron Age hillfort of Quarley Hill, Hampshire, built in the sixth or fifth century BC at the junction of a series of Late Bronze Age linear boundaries. The line of one boundary can be clearly seen running diagonally across the ploughed field.*

nation – and one which might be thought to be somewhat over-complex. All that one can say in defence is that prehistoric systems are likely to have been complex and this explanation has the advantage of being consistent with the observed facts. It is difficult to go further at this stage because of the general paucity of information about the succeeding phase of Iron Age settlement over much of eastern England.

Central southern Britain 800–400 BC

In central southern Britain the evidence is much fuller. The emphasis on ordering and controlling the land which began several centuries earlier continues with the further development of the linear ditch system. The earliest linear ditches, as we have seen, defined blocks of land which were divided into fields. The developed system, which is thought to date to the eighth century, encompassed much larger tracts of land, some of the individual ditches snaking for many kilometres across the landscape (**17**, **18**). That which runs past the Hampshire hillfort of Quarley, for example, can be traced almost continuously for 11km (7 miles) for the most part following the ridge of high land. It is evidently part of a highly complex system of land division which encompasses thousands of hectares of Wessex chalkland. The dating of the system is by no means clear but a recent series of radiocarbon dates suggests that some elements were being dug, or at least recut, in the eighth century. Some ditches cut across earlier coaxial field systems, while elsewhere, most noticeably at Quarley, ditches can be shown to pre-date the construction of early hillforts in the sixth century (see below, p. 34). Taken together, then, the Wessex linear ditch systems were more likely to have been functioning in the eighth century, though in some areas they undoubtedly continued later and may in part have begun earlier.

What the ditches mean is far from clear but at the very least they imply a massive and well-organized reordering of the landscape – a staking out of territorial boundaries on an unprecedented scale.

In several cases the boundaries run towards, and end in, ditched enclosures. One of the best known of these is at Danebury in Hampshire where a linear ditch has been traced for some 2km (1¼ miles) running from the valley of the Test to the hill of Danebury where it ends on a ditched enclosure some 20ha (50 acres) in area. The enclosure differs from the hilltop enclosures described above in that the boundary marker was a ditch: there was no bank, only low dumps of spoil at either lip. A similar example is known on Ladle Hill in northern Hampshire. Here the ditched enclosure was later used to delimit the extent of a hillfort the construction of which was begun but never finished. At Danebury the later hillfort was constructed wholly inside the early enclosure. This coincidence of hillforts with focal points on linear ditch systems is particularly interesting: it is a recurring feature of the Wessex landscape most evident at Quarley and at Sidbury. At the very least it suggests that the linear system still retained a considerable significance into the middle of the sixth century when many of the hillforts of the area began their existence.

Standing back from this somewhat confusing mass of data we can distinguish two distinct phases of activity: the laying out of blocks of coaxial fields in the period c. 1300–900 BC; and the imposition on the landscape of far more extensive territorial divisions some time about 800 BC. The simplest explanation of all this is that we are witnessing a progressive desire to organize the land and therefore to bring its productive capacity under tighter control. Whereas the blocks of fields represent one level of social organization, the linear ditch system

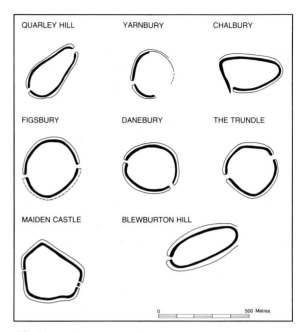

19 *Plans of typical Early Iron Age hillforts of the sixth century BC from Wessex.*

implies a far higher level of centralized control.

Before exploring the implications of all this, it is necessary to take the story of landscape organization one stage further to the period from c. 550 to c. 400 BC when a rash of early hillforts began to appear across the Wessex landscape (**19**). Although a variety of forms exist, many of the early hillforts conform to a standard type consisting of a single bank and ditch following the contour of a hill and enclosing about 5ha (12.5 acres). The bank was frequently, but not invariably, faced externally with vertical timbers or drystone walling and in most cases two entrances were provided at opposite ends of the enclosure. In regions where excavation has been sufficiently extensive it can be shown that early forts were sometimes quite closely spaced. On the Hampshire Wiltshire border, for example, the forts lay between 6 and 14km (4–9 miles) apart.

Excavations at Danebury provide some evidence of what went on within the defences. Here the zone behind the ramparts was densely occupied with circular houses built close to the rampart back. Another group of houses arranged along a road were found in the southern part of the site but much of the rest appears to have been retained as open space where storage pits could be dug, while towards the centre were buildings which may have served as shrines. At Chalbury, in Dorset, field survey and limited excavation showed that here, too, houses, this time of stone, and pits were spread over much of the interior. Other sites have been less extensively examined. While it is, perhaps, unwise to generalize from such a small sample, the overall impression given is that early hillforts were occupied by communities practising a normal range of domestic activities though this does not necessarily imply that occupation was continuous.

The available dating evidence suggests that the early hillforts were built in the late sixth and fifth centuries, usually on or close to sites which had already become focal locations in one of the earlier phases of landscape organization. It could, then, be argued that their construction marked a stage in the developing process of controlling the land. In other words, the forts were a means of demonstrating dominance over the land by a controlling group. Such a contention is impossible to prove but it is consistent with the model which we have been developing earlier.

The full extent of the early hillforts is difficult to define with any precision but they are particularly densely distributed in central southern Britain, extending in a broad band from the south coast to north Wales, with a scatter spreading out along the Chilterns and Northamptonshire uplands. The implication would seem to be that by this time much of the central region was developing a broadly similar socio-economic structure but within this there are likely to have been marked regional differences.

If we look at other aspects of the archaeological record, and in particular pottery, it is possible to explore further the question of developing regional sub-groups of distinctive character. This is particularly clear in Wessex where pottery production was a well-developed skill. In the eighth and seventh centuries there developed an elaborate array of different vessel types, many highly decorated with incised or impressed patterns (**20**). Some were deliberately coated with iron oxide and fired in oxidizing conditions to give a surface which, if well burnished, shone like bronze. The pottery showed a high degree of technical competence while the decoration of the fine wares was little short of exuberant. The distribution of these distinctive types, named after the Wiltshire settlement of All Cannings Cross, is surprisingly wide, stretching from the edge of the Somerset Levels to the eastern borders of Hampshire and from the Solent coast to the crest of the Berkshire Downs, a territory of some 120km (75 miles) from edge to edge.

The similarity of pottery over such a region demonstrates wide-ranging interaction and the acceptance of common values. It implies, at the very least, that the communities within the region were in close contact with each other through a network of exchange systems. Such a view would be entirely consistent with what is known of exchange in bronze which was now at its most intense before the final collapse of the system by the end of the seventh century.

In the sixth and fifth centuries there is

20 *A selection of pots from the Early Iron Age settlement of All Cannings Cross, Wiltshire, dating to the eighth and seventh centuries* BC.

21 *Reconstruction of a house from the Early Iron Age settlement on Cow Down, Longbridge Deverill, Wiltshire. Large houses of this kind are known only in the Early Iron Age in Wessex.*

a marked change in pottery production and distribution: more distinctive types are found confined to much smaller regions. The two most clearly defined groups in Wessex have quite separate distributions, one centring on what is now southern Wiltshire, the other on southern Dorset. The implication is that, now, smaller social groups were beginning to distinguish themselves and it is surely no coincidence that this happens in the period when large numbers of early hillforts are built across the face of the landscape.

If we are correct in seeing the long-term changes in the socio-economic development of central southern Britain as driven by the desire to establish a greater control over land and its agrarian product, then the collapse of the bronze exchange networks in the seventh century might well have increased the urgency for the individual groups to stake out their territorial demands. The building of hillforts in dominant focal locations should be seen against this background. The break-up of 'greater Wessex' into smaller social groupings after about 600 BC, hinted at by the pottery evidence, would fit well with our model of increasing territoriality. Setting out the lines of argument in this detail enables the reader better to appreciate the strengths – and weaknesses – of archaeological interpretation.

The position of the elite in this period of transformation is unclear. One possibility is that it was they who caused the hillforts to be built for their own aggrandizement and protection but there is no firm evidence of this. A more likely possibility is that they lived in farmsteads in the countryside around – places like Little Woodbury, Cow Down and Pimperne in all three of which circular timber houses of monumental proportions have been found (**21**). If this were so then it would allow that the hillforts, at this stage at least, provided a centralizing focus for the activities of the larger social community. The subsequent development of this system will be considered in the next chapter.

North-eastern Britain 800–400 BC

Turning now to the north-east of Britain, from the North York Moors to the southern foothills of the Grampians, we find a situation which has both similarities and differences to the centre south and the south-east – real differences born of the more northerly upland landscape and apparent differences caused by a more partial archaeological record.

The situation in the Late Bronze Age is obscure. In the more upland regions, where the evidence is best preserved, clusters of huts lying unenclosed amid small fields cleared out of the waste are a recurrent feature, but it is difficult to be sure whether they constitute the only settlement form or are simply a specialized response to the utilization of the upland fringe – perhaps the summer bothies used by one segment of the population whose homes lie undiscovered in the lowlands. It is as well to remember that various forms of transhumant farming were, until recently, a widespread feature of peasant Europe. Some larger settlements are known, as for example Eildon Hill North in the old county of Roxburghshire where a hilltop up to ¹/₂km (¹/₄ mile) in diameter was enclosed by an earthwork within which many hundreds of hut circles can be detected. The trial excavations, recently undertaken, suggest a Late Bronze Age date for some at least. How to interpret such a complex is difficult without far more evidence but in many characteristics Eildon is similar to the hilltop enclosures of central southern Britain and may have served a centralizing function in the agrarian cycle, the hut circles implying a period of residence if only for a few months during the year.

As in the south a major change can be observed in the seventh century when a new type of settlement emerges to be found widely across the whole region, though with minor variations from place to place. The essential features of this new settlement form are an enclosing close-set timber palisade, sometimes double, with one or more large circular houses

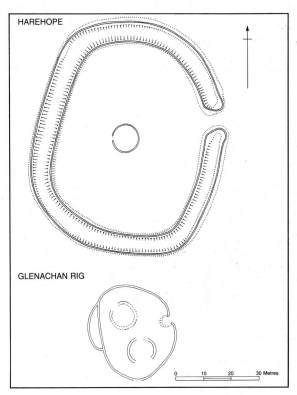

22 *Two palisaded enclosures from northern Britain to demonstrate the variation in size and, presumably, in status.*

within (**22**, **23**). One of the largest of these sites, White Hill in Peebleshire, is only 0.7ha (1.75 acres) in extent. Some retain evidence of many houses but no more than one or two need have been in use at any one time. These palisaded enclosures are therefore likely to have represented family units.

The conspicuous consumption of timber used to make the palisades and the dominant nature of the principal centrally placed houses, which were frequently in excess of 10m (*c.* 30ft) in diameter, were clearly meant to impress. These settlements were redolent of power and dominance and are therefore equivalent in many ways to the elite farmsteads and the hillforts of central southern Britain.

North-western Britain 800–400 BC

The face of the north-western region, from the Firth of Clyde to the Shetlands, is varied in the

23 *The settlement of Clickhimin was built on an island in a loch on the Island of Shetland.*

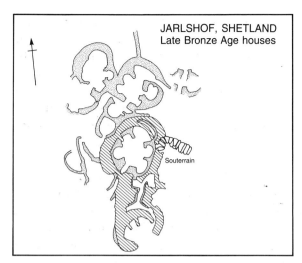

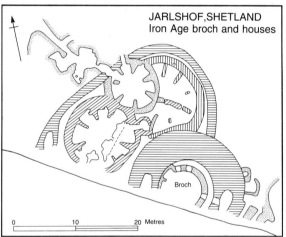

24 *The settlement of Jarlshof, Shetland, contrasting the small cellular houses of the Late Bronze Age with the larger, free-standing, round houses of the Iron Age.*

extreme, its overriding characteristics being its wet Atlantic climate and the dissected maritime-dominated nature of the landscape.

In the Late Bronze Age the principal settlement form was the cellular, stone-built house set deep in the soil in semi-subterranean fashion to provide protection for the inhabitants of the harsh climate. Houses of this kind began to be built in the Neolithic period and at Jarlshof (**24**) and Clickhimin, both on Shetland, were still being constructed in the eighth century BC. The period 750–500 saw a dramatic change: the appearance of a new type of house – upstanding stone-built round houses of the kind excavated on Orkney at Bu, Pierowall and Quanterness. So striking is the change that some writers believe it to have been the result of a new incoming elite. However, once inside the house the arrangement, with its central service area containing the hearth and with compartments opening off, would have been entirely familiar to someone used to living in an earlier cellular house. In other words, while the message given by the structure was different its social implications were not. These early round houses, in contrast to the cellular structures, were visible and dominant. As in the case

of the palisaded enclosures in the north-eastern zone they were meant to be seen and to impress. And like the palisaded enclosures they lie at the beginning of an enduring and developing tradition.

A perspective

In the brief span of this chapter we have stressed the rich and variable nature of the evidence for this crucial period of transition when the old cycle – the Neolithic-Bronze Age mode of exploitation of the landscape, with its emphasis on large monuments as a form of social expression (the huge collective tombs and the religious monuments like Avebury and Stonehenge) – gave way to a new cycle, the overriding characteristic of which was the dominance of the individual, or better the lineage (group of related families), over the land. The new type of usually dominant domestic architecture which developed at this time over much of the British Isles symbolized the change.

In some areas, like the north-east and the north-west and the whole of the Atlantic west, the individual family, or extended family, was the unit of dominance. There is little evidence for the communal activities of larger social agglomerations. In contrast, in central southern Britain, the organization of the landscape, with its linear ditches, hilltop enclosures and early hillforts, shows all the signs of a higher level of social complexity. By the fifth century the distinctive pottery distributions could be taken to imply the formation of distinct tribes. The development of the eastern zone is, at present, problematic after the period between 1100–700 BC when the circular enclosures of the elite reached their peak. Evidence is sparse – though there are hints in the very scrappy data that larger agglomerations of village size may have begun to emerge. If so the contrast with the rest of Britain is interesting and deserves more thorough investigation.

The great transition thus created entirely new landscapes and set in motion a developing social complexity which was to characterize the rest of the British Iron Age.

4

Conflicting claims:
the emergence of tribal entities

The period from about 400 BC until the end of the second century, which can conveniently be called the Middle Iron Age, saw the emergence of very distinct regional differences among the communities of the British Isles: it was also a time when the population showed signs of rapid expansion. Population growth among prehistoric societies is notoriously difficult to demonstrate and virtually impossible to quantify but wherever intensive field surveys have been carried out in Britain the number of Middle Iron Age settlements identified usually exceeds, sometimes considerably, the number of earlier sites. The consistency of the pattern, which is particularly clear in central southern Britain, is sufficient to suggest that population increase is likely to have been a significant factor lying behind the development of society during this period.

Another important generalization which must be made at this stage is that the productive systems of society underwent a process of intensification. Quite simply Middle Iron Age sites yield far more artefacts and debris than do Early Iron Age sites. Superficially this might seem to be a trivial observation but it is most certainly not so. It implies a growing intensity not only in general productivity but also an increasing complexity in the social and economic systems which governed production and exchange – in other words life was becoming richer, more varied, and more complex. It is a point to which we shall return (pp. 52).

The data available for the study of the Middle Iron Age are varied. In the south and east of Britain hundreds of settlements are known and a significant percentage have been excavated, at least in part. In this area pottery is plentiful and because fashions in pottery decoration seem to have changed quite quickly it is possible to use pottery as a means of phasing sites. Distributions of similar decorative motifs on pottery also provide a way of approaching the question of emerging ethnic identities. In parts of the west and the north, where pottery is rarer and less elaborate, dating and the definition of regional groupings is more difficult, though an increasing number of radiocarbon dates are helping to structure the data. The rich and varied evidence available for Britain at this time makes it one of the most thoroughly researched parts of prehistoric Europe.

The Atlantic zone and the tin trade

The Roman poet Avienus working in the fourth century AD wrote a poem called *Ora Maritima* (The Maritime Shores) in which he utilized an early sailing manual describing the Atlantic sea-ways, compiled in the sixth century BC probably by a mariner based at Massilia (Marseilles). The Massiliote Periplus, as it is known, describes the routes used by Tartessian and Phoenician traders along the Atlantic coasts from Cadiz northwards to Brittany, Ireland and Britain and is the first text to refer to the exchange systems known otherwise only from archaeological evidence. That such a sailing manual existed is a clear indication of the growing importance of the Atlantic trade routes to Mediterranean society. Towards the end of the fourth century we hear again of the western routes when a Greek sailor, Pytheas, journeyed through the Straits of Gibraltar, sailing northwards to Brittany and beyond.

The motive for these journeys, and no doubt many others, was to explore and to exploit the metal resources of these regions and in particular the tin which was to be had in Galicia (north-western Iberia), Brittany and in south-western Britain.

A later writer, Diodorus Siculus, basing his remarks upon now-lost writings of Posidonius, provides a fascinating insight into details of this trade. He mentions the peninsula of *Belerium* (i.e. the extreme south-west of Britain) where tin was found. It was, he said, worked into knuckle-bone-sized ingots and taken to an island called Ictis just off the British shore,

> at ebb-tide the space between the island and the mainland becomes dry and they can take the tin in large quantities over to the island on their wagons.... On the island of Ictis the merchants purchase tin from the natives... where it is taken to Gaul and overland to the Mediterranean.

Further details are added by Pliny, quoting an earlier source Timaeus. He mentions an island called Mictis, 'six days sail from Britain' where tin is to be had and to which the Britons cross in 'boats of osier covered with stitched hides'.

These two texts have given rise to a lively debate as to whether Ictis is Mictis and if so what 'six days sail from Britain' can possibly mean, given the description of Ictis by Diodorus. Such speculation is worthless since the scraps of text which have come down to us are fragmentary, garbled and open to many interpretations. All we can safely say is that they reflect an organized exchange in tin between Atlantic traders and the inhabitants of south-west Britain. The reference to British skin boats

provides an interesting insight into methods of transport at the time and is a reminder that these maritime communities were well adapted to their environment.

Some archaeological reflections of these trading patterns are to be found in the south-west. Brooches from Mount Batten near Plymouth and Harlyn Bay on the north coast of Cornwall, though quite probably of local manufacture, resemble types current in the fifth and fourth centuries in Aquitania and northern Iberia. There is also an enigmatic bronze figurine from Aust in the Severn estuary which is closely similar to Iberian figurines from Andalucia (**25**). Another, of the same general type, was found at Sligo in Ireland. To this rather meagre list may be added a number of coins of Mediterranean origin found scattered across southern Britain, some at least of which are likely to have been brought to Britain at the time (though many may be much later imports). Material of this kind may come from among the exchange goods which the traders offered to the Britons in return for their tin.

The picture sketched from the scraps of text

25 *The small bronze figurine from Aust, Gloucestershire, (no. 1) is probably an import from Iberia. It may be compared with one found near Granada in Andalucia (no. 2).*

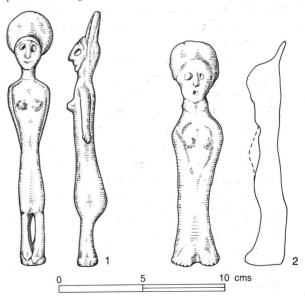

26 (above) Decorated bronze vessel (or vessels) from a cist at Cerrig y Drudion, Clwyd: a fine example of insular 'Celtic' art. The original reconstruction, as a hanging bowl, is no longer thought to be likely.

and the scatter of exotic items is necessarily grossly over-simplified. In reality there must have been a complex network of exchange mechanisms which bound the maritime communities of the Atlantic seaboard. By far the greatest bulk of material moving along these routes would have done so in cycles of gift exchange between neighbouring communities, and direct contact with traders from the south is likely to have been comparatively rare. There is no way, however, in which we can reasonably quantify this.

The intensity of contact between the southwest and Armorica is reflected not so much in the presence of imported artefacts as in similarities of culture. This is perhaps most dramatically displayed in the use of decorative motifs common to La Tène art. The so-called

27 (right) Metal vessels and their ceramic copies. Bronze cups: no. 1 from Keshcarrigan, Co. Leitrim, Ireland, and no. 2 from Rose Ash, Devon. The ceramic copies are Breton: no. 3 from Blavet, Hénon, Côtes d'Armor, and no. 4 from Hennebont, Côtes d'Armor.

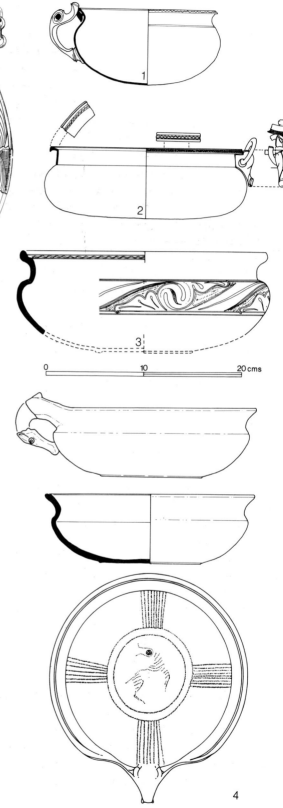

28 *The Cornish cliff castle of The Rumps, St Minver, Cornwall. The form and location is typical of sites in south-west Wales, Cornwall and Brittany.*

bronze 'hanging bowl' (more likely to be a lid), found in a stone cist at Cerrig y Drudion in north Wales, is ornamented with a range of sophisticated curvilinear motifs of a kind particularly popular for decorating fine pottery in Brittany (**26**). It is probably no accident that it was the south-west British communities who developed the most original decorated pottery in the whole of Britain. A shared delight in the exuberance of curvilinear decoration is likely to have resulted from the exchange of decorated items between the social elite. If so the medium is most likely to have been bronze work. This is particularly vividly demonstrated by the fine animal-headed bronze bowls from Rose Ash in Devon and Keshcarrigan (Co. Leitrim) in Ireland (**27**). Both were of closely similar form and represent a type comparatively well known in western Britain. The actual form of the bowls was copied by potters in Brittany, one of whom even reproduced the animal-head handle on a vessel found at Hennebont in the Côtes

d'Armor. The same type of animal-headed vessel, but made in wood, was found in an Irish bog in Co. Armagh. Here, then, we see a basic idea, probably developed in the first instance by a school of metalworkers, copied in other media over a wide area from Armorica to Ireland.

Other aspects of culture serve to link Armorica, south-western Britain, south-west Wales, and southern Ireland. The fortified, sea-girt promontories – the so-called 'cliff castles' – are found in all areas (**28**) while the most common form of settlement across the whole region is the embanked enclosure of the type known as the *rath* or *round*. The use of underground storage chambers, called souterrains in Brittany and fogous in Cornwall, is a further shared characteristic. Settlement features of this kind, of course, reflect similarities in socio-economic systems which are to some extent conditioned by similar environments. Nevertheless the strong probability remains that constant contacts between the disparate regions served to encourage a degree of parallel development.

Many thousands of earthwork-enclosed settlements cover the landscape of Cornwall,

43

29 *Reconstruction of the Early Iron Age house excavated at Carn Euny, Cornwall.*

Devon and south Wales and several have been excavated (**29**, **30**) on a large enough scale to suggest that they represent the homesteads of family units. Variation in status no doubt occurred and was probably reflected in the size of the earthworks, the complexity of their gates,

30 *Reconstruction of the later Iron Age stone-built house at Carn Euny, Cornwall.*

the number of circuits of enclosing earthworks and access to rare commodities like glass, beads and bracelets. If so, then the category referred to as **multiple enclosure forts** might be regarded as settlements of the elite (**31**). The majority of these are sited on hillsides within easy reach of well-watered pastures which indicate that cattle rearing may have played a significant part in the economy.

Kent, the Thames estuary and East Anglia

The proximity of the extreme south-east corner of Britain to the Continent will have ensured that the Straits of Dover served to join the two regions, the Thames and the Somme, providing convenient routes to the hinterlands. Comparatively little is yet known of the communities occupying these coastal zones, though a number of sites have been located and sampled. What does emerge, however, are close similarities between the ceramic development on the two sides of the Channel.

A group of pottery found many years ago at Eastbourne, with painted lozenge decoration on high-shouldered jars, mirrors Continental fashions of the sixth century BC, though the Eastbourne vessels were locally made (**32**). More recently it has been possible to recognize a distinctive, rusticated type of pottery, quite widely distributed east of the river Medway, which has developed locally in parallel with similar styles on the adjacent Continent; and from two of the Kentish sites, Highstead and Dollands Moor, fine shouldered bowls decorated with geometric designs painted in haematite have been recovered (**32**). These lie within a tradition of painted wares widely distributed in northern France. Such scraps of evidence are sufficient to demonstrate the reality of the links between the two areas, though the nature of the interaction is impossible yet to define.

In the Thames Valley, and extending through East Anglia to the Wash, there developed a distinctive assemblage of pottery which included sharp-shouldered bowls sometimes

31 *The multivallate, hill-slope enclosure of Tregeare Round, St Kew, Cornwall. The central enclosure was probably where the main habitation lay. The outer enclosures may have been for stock.*

32 *Pottery of the fifth and fourth centuries BC from eastern Britain in the style of Continental types. Top: painted vessel from Eastbourne, Sussex copying western European Hallstatt types. Bottom: painted vessels from Dollards Moor, Kent, possibly imported from northern Gaul in the fourth century.*

with low pedestal bases and coarse ware jars with their surfaces covered with finger impressions. Both types can be paralleled among the pottery assemblages found on the adjacent Continent from northern France to southern Holland, and indeed the similarities across the North Sea are more impressive than between this group and, say, Wessex. While, in the past, this kind of observation has led to suggestions of 'invasions' from Europe, it is more likely that we are simply observing the archaeological reflection of long and well-established contacts involving networks of exchange.

We know little, yet, of the settlements of eastern England in the Middle Iron Age but the scraps of evidence at present available suggest that large agglomerations of village size may be the norm. If so then the similarity with the adjacent Continent would be further reinforced.

The Arras Culture of Yorkshire

The north-east of England, from the Humber estuary to the Vale of Pickering, constitutes a culturally distinct zone characterized by a distinctive burial rite found nowhere else in

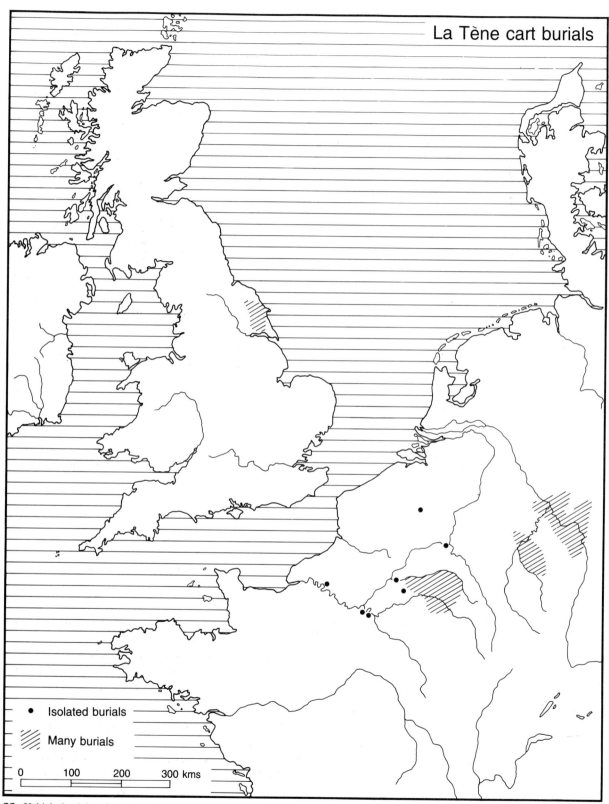

La Tène cart burials

• Isolated burials

/// Many burials

0   100   200   300 kms

33 *Vehicle burials of the fifth to third centuries* BC *in Britain and the adjacent Continent.*

WETWANG

Burial 1

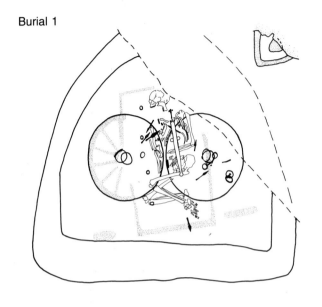

Burial 2

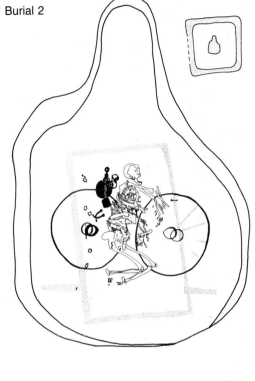

Burial 3

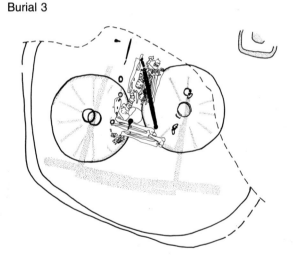

0   1   2 Metres

34 *Vehicle burials from the Yorkshire cemetery at Wetwang Slack (see also* **9***).*

Britain. The group is usually referred to as the Arras Culture after one of the cemetery sites discovered last century.

The burial practices of the Arras Culture involve three distinct characteristics: the development of large cemeteries often of many hundreds of graves; the definition of the individual grave mound by a surrounding rectangular ditched enclosure; and an elite burial tradition involving the interment of a two-wheeled vehicle with the body. The grave goods, frequently accompanying the dead, reflect the status of the deceased.

It has long been realized that the Arras Culture burials have much in common with several distinct groups of La Tène burials in northern Europe where the burial of a vehicle was an indication of status (**9**, **33**, **34**). Indeed the only significant difference between the British and the Continental traditions is that the Yorkshire rite did not use fine pottery as an accompaniment to the rich interments. As

47

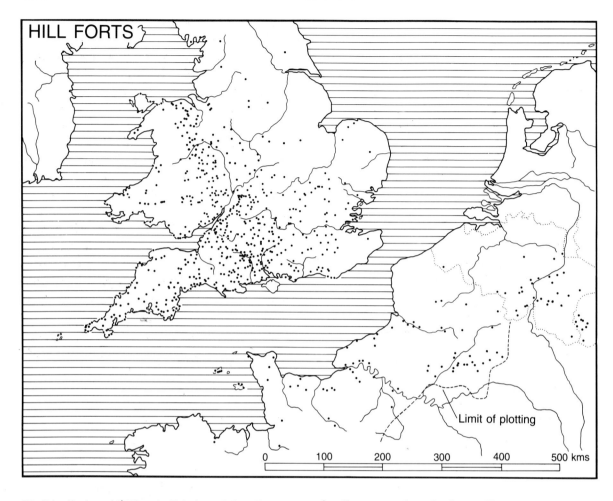

35 *Distribution of hillforts in Britain and the adjacent Continent emphasizing the unusually dense clustering in central southern Britain where, unlike most other regions, hillforts continued to develop in the Middle Iron Age.*

we have mentioned above, these similarities have been used to support the view that the Arras Culture owed its origins to the arrival of high-status newcomers, coming from northern France or Belgium, into the Humber region some time in the fifth century BC. While this must still remain a possibility, some writers have suggested that the phenomenon can equally well be explained as the emulation of exotic, 'foreign' behaviour by indigenous elites striving to distinguish themselves. Both explanations are equally possible and it is unlikely that archaeological evidence will ever be able,

finally, to resolve the issue. Even so the implication remains that in the fifth century, if only for a brief period, the communities of the Yorkshire Wolds had developed a close contact with their neighbours across the North Sea.

The settlement pattern of the region is one of straggling village-like communities set in an organized landscape of ditched fields linked by roadways. The parallels here seem to be with the more southerly regions of eastern England rather than with the north-east.

Central southern Britain

The amount of data relevant to Middle Iron Age settlement in central southern Britain is considerable. The overwhelming impression it gives is that, while continuity was the prime factor, the social and economic systems which governed the community underwent massive intensification, which resulted in the emergence of a far more complex society than that of the earlier period. This is particularly clear with regard to hillforts (**35**). As a generalization it can be said that, in areas where early hillforts had already developed, a few of the early sites continued in use and were frequently strengthened or enlarged while the rest were abandoned. In other words certain locations, which we can designate as **developed hillforts**, emerged as central places at the expense of others (**36**).

The developed hillforts sometimes adopted exactly the same defensive circuit as their earlier predecessors as, for example, at Danebury, but at other locations (e.g. Maiden Castle) the old circuits were only partially used, the area enclosed being extended, while in a few cases like Yarnbury in Wiltshire the old defences were abandoned altogether and an entirely new, more extensive line was adopted. For the most part the ramparts were dump-constructed, that is with no element of vertical walling fronting them. In some cases multiple lines of bank and ditch were constructed reaching their most elaborate in examples like Maiden Castle and Hambledon Hill in Dorset.

36 *A selection of plans of developed hillforts emphasizing the considerable variation in size that occurs. The shaded areas represent the initial, earlier, enclosure from which the forts developed.*

YARNBURY

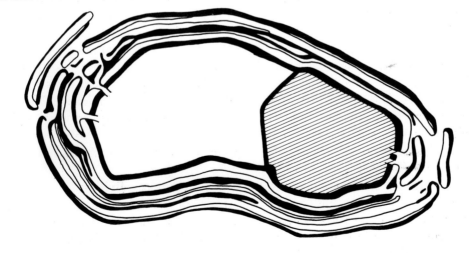

TORBERRY

MAIDEN CASTLE

0   600 Metres

37 *Danebury, Hampshire, a typical developed hillfort of Wessex, during excavation.*

in the Middle Iron Age. This need not, of course, imply an actual movement of people.

A number of developed hillforts have now been subjected to quite large-scale excavation with the result that much has been learned of their functions in the period *c.* 400–100 BC. Among these we can list Danebury and Bury Hill in Hampshire, Maiden Castle in Dorset, South Cadbury in Somerset and Croft Ambrey, Midsummer Hill and Credenhill in the Welsh Borderlands. All have provided evidence of intense occupation with structures of various kinds being renewed time and time again on the same plots.

The evidence is at its fullest at Danebury where over 57 per cent of the interior has now been excavated (**37**, **38**, **39**, **colour plate 8**). One of the most striking features of the plan is a branching pattern of roads spreading out from the main east gate, with a wider 'main' road leading across the centre of the fort to the site of the south-west gate which had been blocked by this time. South of the main road

38 *One of the houses inside Danebury. The wall was constructed of wattlework, with a drainage gully outside. The approach was metalled with trampled chalk.*

Another characteristic of the majority of the developed hillforts is the complexity of their entrance earthworks (**72**). The overall result of these changes was to create sites, the very appearance of which was redolent of power and a dominance over the surrounding landscape. While there can be no reasonable doubt that the forts were designed to have a considerable defensive capacity, the proliferation of earthworks at some of the sites was far in excess of military needs – in short the forts were a symbol of the prestige of the community while at the same time providing protection when required.

In some areas hillforts of developed type were constructed on virgin sites. This seems to be true of most of the sites along the North Downs, in the northern part of the Weald, and also of certain sites in Devon. The implication here might be that the social system, of which the hillfort formed an essential element, spread outwards from the core area of the centre south

39 *The interior of the hillfort of Danebury showing the density of features (mainly storage pits and post-holes) and the dendritic pattern of roads.*

were rows of four- and six-post storage buildings aligned along roads, while in the northern part of the fort a subsidiary road led from the east gate to a group of rectangular structures identified as shrines. There are also suggestions that this central area may have been occupied by large circular houses but the evidence is fragmentary. Around the periphery of the fort, close against the back of the rampart, was a heavily utilized zone of houses, storage structures, pits and open working yards.

Many of the characteristics of this Danebury complex can be found at the other, less extensively excavated sites. Shrines are known or suspected at South Cadbury and Maiden Castle and at both there is ample evidence of dense and continuous occupation behind the ramparts. The Welsh Borderland hillforts of Croft

Ambrey, Midsummer Hill and Credenhill all have clear traces of rows of rectangular post-built structures. Taken together it is reasonable to suppose that the picture presented by Danebury was representative of many, if not all, of the developed hillforts of the central southern region. It would be quite wrong, however, to suggest that all developed hillforts were of the same status – the huge input of labour into Maiden Castle must place it on an entirely different social level to, say, the very much smaller enclosure of Torberry in Sussex, even though Torberry, with its massively constructed entrance, shares the general characteristics of developed hillforts.

The array of material recovered from developed hillforts like Danebury appears to be little different in quality from that which is found in contemporary settlement sites, but in quantity, area for area, hillforts are far more prolific – an observation which reflects upon intensity of activity. This similarity of assemblage would suggest that the activities normally carried out at settlement sites were also undertaken within the forts – spinning, weaving, leatherwork, carpentry and metalworking, etc. There are, however, some apparent differences of considerable interest. Danebury, for example, has produced a collection of well-made stone weights which seem to conform to certain weight standards. This would suggest that careful measurement may have been carried out at the fort. Moreover, ingots of iron, in the form of sword-shaped currency bars, and fragments of clay containers used to import salt from the coast, imply that raw materials may have been brought to the site in bulk possibly to be redistributed. Evidence of this kind is open to various interpretations but it does support the view, favoured here, that one of the functions of developed hillforts was to provide centres where a range of locally produced commodities could be stored and used in exchange for rare raw materials such as salt and iron brought in from outside the territory. The very considerable storage capacity implied by the rows of storage structures found in several of the forts indicates the amassing of surpluses. Over much of the centre south these are most likely to have been grain and wool.

Like the hillforts, the non-hillfort settlement of the Middle Iron Age frequently developed without significant break from earlier settlements. Many were enclosed within boundary ditches backed, presumably, by hedges, but some, like the settlement at Winnall Down in Hampshire, outgrew the confines of their silted-up ditches, while others seem always to have been without well-defined boundaries. The variety is not surprising. It reflects the histories of the individual settlements, their status and changing fortunes as well as differences in economies resulting from the character of the ecological zone in which the individual settlements lay. The overall impression, however, is that, with few exceptions, the settlements of the centre south were those of family or extended-family groups.

Towards the end of the Middle Iron Age new settlement types begin to appear. The most enigmatic are the so-called 'banjo enclosures' – small circular ditched enclosures of less than a hectare in area approached by a long causeway defined by ditches on either side (**40**). These were originally thought to be cattle enclosures but the few examined by excavation have produced evidence of occupation continuing through the Late Iron Age. In Hampshire, where the type is particularly well represented, a significant number continued in use into the Roman period and eventually evolved into

40 *A banjo enclosure under excavation at Nettlebank Copse, Hampshire.*

small Roman villas. One possibility is that they were settlements of some status and remained in the hands of the minor elite who, after the invasion, gradually acquired the trappings of Romanization. The continuity of land holding which this implies, spanning 300–400 years, is particularly interesting.

The second group of settlements to appear towards the end of the Middle Iron Age are large circular enclosures defended by one or two massive ditches of hillfort proportions. Very little is yet known of them but the amount of labour invested in the boundary earthworks suggests a desire to impress – perhaps here we are seeing the emergence of elites setting up new territorial claims as pressure on land intensified. To this same general category belongs the so-called hillfort of Bury Hill II, near Andover. Here, long after an early hillfort had gone out of use, a new circular enclosure was constructed, defended by a substantial ditch with banks inside and out. Excavations have shown that the enclosure was occupied, though by no means as extensively as the nearby hillfort of Danebury. What is particularly interesting is that the animal bone assemblages from the two sites differed noticeably – Danebury was dominated by sheep while at Bury Hill horses were unusually prominent – an observation given greater relevance by the discovery of quantities of bronze horse trappings, some of them elaborately décorated. It is tempting to suggest that Bury Hill II, which dates to the late second century BC, was constructed by a rival group, within what had been Danebury territory, whose economic base was markedly, possibly deliberately, different from that of the traditional centre.

Sufficient will have been said to show that the Middle Iron Age in central southern Britain was a time of change. From among the many long-established social foci a few continued to serve the community as increasingly strongly defended developed hillforts, where, if we are correct, a range of functions was carried out: storage of society's surplus, the exchange and redistribution of commodities, religious observances, etc. In this model each fort will have been the centre of a carefully defined territory. By this time the landscape around was densely settled, in some areas with habitation sites every kilometre or so, and there are indications that settlement density was increasing. The emergence of new strongly defended sites towards the end of the period and sporadic evidence of violent death and destruction (pp. 93–4) are clear indications of a society in a state of increasing stress.

The north-eastern zone

The north-eastern zone, from the North York Moors to the southern foothills of the Scottish Highlands, developed a highly distinctive character during the Middle Iron Age as the landscape became covered with a rash of 'hillforts'. The use of the phrase 'hillfort' in this zone is confusing since the vast majority of the 1500 or so defended enclosures are less than a hectare in extent and in the south would not be regarded as belonging to the same category as hillforts. There are, in fact, only 14 or so sites of hillfort proportions in the region and there is no convincing evidence that any of them were extensively used or defended in this period. The north-east, then, is a territory of fortified homesteads (**41**) and not a hillfort-dominated zone.

A number of excavations within the region have shown that many of these Middle Iron Age farmsteads enclosed by one or sometimes two circuits of banks and ditches developed out of earlier palisaded enclosures. At Huckhoe, in Northumberland, for example, the earthworks were built immediately after the palisaded settlement was destroyed by fire some time in the sixth century. But the earthwork enclosures at two other Northumberland sites, Borough Law and Ingram Hill, were not built until the third century BC. Some enclosures seem to have been constantly remodelled. Such was Broxmouth hillfort in East Lothian: here a comparatively small enclosure was rebuilt on

41 *A fortified homestead at Warden Hill, Northumberland.*

five separate occasions, the complexity of its entrance earthworks suggesting that it was a settlement of high status.

Clearly, over such a vast territory and during three centuries or so of development the pattern varied but the overall trend towards the creation of earthwork enclosures is both widespread and consistent. The fact that so many were simply remodellings of existing palisaded settlements is an indication of the essential social continuity characteristic of the time. If we are correct in suggesting that the change from the Late Bronze Age style of settlement to the palisaded homestead marked a change of attitude, the homestead now being regarded as a symbol of dominance over the land, then the 'monumentalizing' of it with ditches and earthworks may have represented another stage in the same general process which linked the control of the land to status and used the settlement as the outward and visible sign of this. It may even be that size and complexity of the enclosing earthworks and the elaboration of the entrances directly reflected status and was rigorously controlled by social convention –

much as it was in Ireland or in Saxon England in the first millennium AD.

North-western zone

The north-western zone of the British Isles is dominated by a variety of stone-built homesteads which can be divided, very approximately, between the duns of the west and the brochs of the north but both typologically and distributionally there is considerable overlap. A great deal has been written about the origins and development of these structures – far more than the actual hard evidence would justify – but the general view, accepted by the majority of archaeologists, is that the brochs and duns represent an indigenous development in a zone where timber was rare but stone everywhere to be had.

The comparatively recent demonstration that stone-built round houses began in the Early Iron Age has helped to clarify ideas about development in the north-west, and the picture which now emerges is of a gradual elaboration and aggrandizement of the round house concept after about 400 BC leading to the evolution of **complex round houses**, of which the broch is one type. Early brochs of the Middle Iron Age like Crosskirk in Caithness, Howe on Orkney (**42**) and Jarlshof on Shetland all showed refinements such as intramural cells and internally projecting ledges, associated roofing or gallery construction, but they had not yet developed the tower-like proportions which characterized a few of the later brochs like the famous structure on the island of Mousa off mainland Shetland. At both Howe and Jarlshof the walls of outer enclosures abutted the broch, while at Crosskirk ancillary buildings were erected outside at an early stage in the development. In all these demonstrably early sites the complex round house was the centre of a larger settlement complex, which at Gurness and Midhowe on Orkney eventually

42 *Two Orkney brochs each forming the central elements of tightly clustered settlements within protective stone walls.*

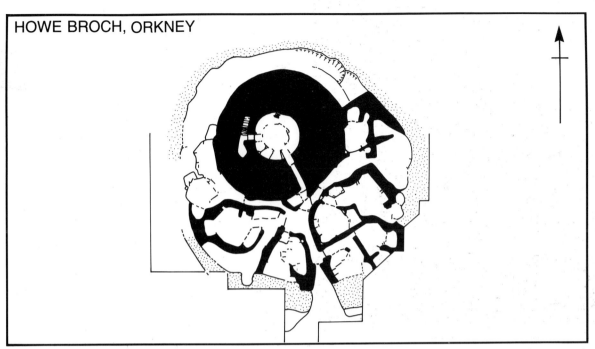

HOWE BROCH, ORKNEY

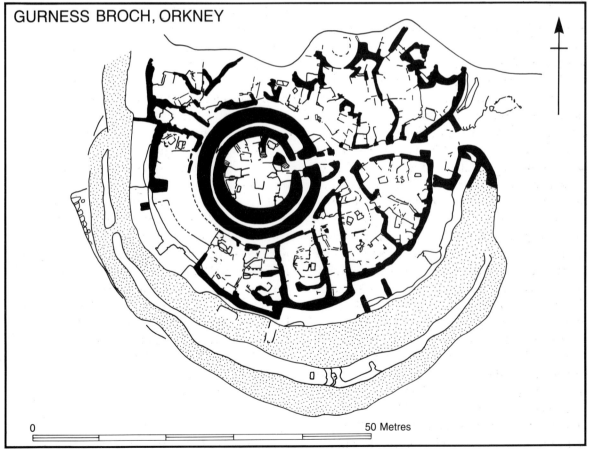

GURNESS BROCH, ORKNEY

0   50 Metres

43 *The Broch of Gurness, Orkney, is sited close to the shore. It commands the rich fishing resources of Rousey Sound, the cultivatable soils of the coastal zone and the grazing of the inland moor.*

developed into village-like proportions. At Gurness (**43, colour plate 2**) it is estimated that there was space for between 30 and 40 families in the late first century BC or early first century AD.

There can be little doubt that the broch and the dun were constructed to impress – they were practically and symbolically centres of power providing a visual focus legitimizing the lineages who built and occupied them. Each will have had its own distinctive history and it remains a strong possibility that some declined or were abandoned as others rose to dominance, encouraging a coalescence of population in their shadows.

This brief survey of Middle Iron Age settlement across the British Isles shows that, in spite of the considerable variety in settlement form,

many areas underwent very similar development. Settlements seem to have become more numerous with time as the population grew and the landscape filled up and everywhere, except perhaps in the east of England, the emphasis was on the construction of the permanent and visually dominant homestead. But only in the central southern zone, with the emergence of developed hillforts, do we find physical evidence of a more complex and centralized form of social system emerging. What happened in the eastern zone is at present more difficult to say. The scattered village-like settlement and elaborate cemeteries of the Yorkshire Wolds reflect a very different kind of social system. Indeed the huge cemeteries laid out along trackways suggest an attitude to the community, and perhaps even to the ownership of land, which finds no counterpart anywhere else in Britain. Our understanding of the south-east must await more evidence.

The emergence of tribal groupings

When the Romans invaded Britain in AD 43

they found a country divided into a number of tribal groupings: some of them they adopted as the basis of their own administrative system. It is, however, wrong to assume that these 'tribes' implied a close regional harmony. Many of those in the south may have been socially cohesive, but in the north it is far more likely that the names recorded were those of powerful lineages to whom the widely-spread population owed some degree of allegiance.

The tribes of the south-east were minting distinctive coins at the time of the invasion, a fact which indicates some kind of socio-economic unity. These tribal coinages can be traced back to the middle of the first century BC or in some cases a decade or two earlier. The question then is how far back can 'tribal' groupings be recognized in the archaeological record?

One way to approach the question is by considering the distribution patterns of distinctive pottery styles, assuming that pottery decoration reflects ethnic division. Fig. **44** offers a summary of the relevant evidence for central southern Britain. The territories indicated by pottery groupings of the sixth to fifth century are still distinguishable in the fourth to second century – by which time a rather more complex pattern had developed. There is also a degree of overlap between this and the wider pottery distributions of the late first century BC and early first century AD which can themselves be related to the distribution patterns of the tribal coinages. It is tempting, therefore, to suggest that some of the zones favouring particular styles of pottery decoration, distinguishable as early as the sixth to fifth century, retained a degree of separate identity throughout the Iron Age – to emerge, sometimes combined into larger units, as components in the tribal system which the Romans encountered.

44 *The emergence of tribal zones in southern Britain. The maps demonstrate a strong continuity in regional groupings based on the distribution of distinctive pottery styles, stretching from the sixth century BC until the first century AD by which time named tribes had emerged.*

It is interesting to note that the region where the pottery styles are clearest – central southern Britain – is just that area where the settlement pattern evidence suggests the development of a complex social system based on territorial units dominated by developed hillforts. Taken together it does seem as though the communities

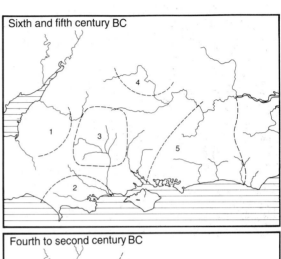

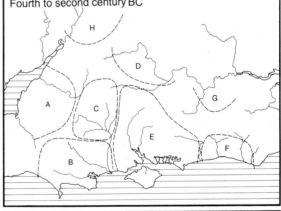

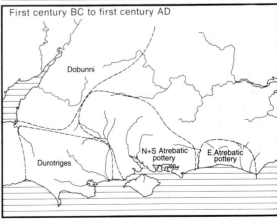

45 *The White Horse of Uffington probably dates originally to the Iron Age. It was cut on the north-facing slope of the Berkshire Downs close to a hillfort and may have been a territorial marker. (See also* **colour plate 4**.*)*

of central southern Britain, possibly by virtue of the sheer density of population, began to develop a regional coherence early in the Iron Age which led to the emergence of distinct tribes or confederations (**45**). No doubt there were other equally cohesive units elsewhere in Britain like the Arras Culture of the Yorkshire Wolds that emerged into history as the Parisi. In this region the fact that social and economic development was continuous from the fifth century would suggest that the tribal identity can be traced back at least that far.

In other areas of the west and north, where the settlement pattern is more dispersed and the social unit was the extended family, a network of relationships will have developed by intermarriage, creating patchworks of social interdependence. These groupings, in say the south-west peninsula – now Devon and Cornwall – may have recognized their difference from communities further east and may even have considered themselves to have been men of Dumnonia, but this does not necessarily mean that they recognized a unifying authority – the constraints of geography in these remote regions may have been sufficient to give the appearance of unity.

For Britain, then, the Middle Iron Age (400–100 BC) was a time of developing intensity. Man's impact on the land increased and as populations grew so the network of social and ethnic allegiances crystallized into a more formal structure. The scene was set for the final transformation – the prelude to the Roman invasion.

5

Reformation and tribal society

To understand the dramatic changes which came about in south-east Britain after the middle of the second century BC, it is necessary to broaden our horizons to encompass western Europe and the western Mediterranean. The second half of the second century BC was a time of rapid social and economic change in the west Mediterranean. Rome had already gained possession of the larger islands – Sicily, Corsica and Sardinia – and was now establishing her rule firmly on the scattered and somewhat recalcitrant communities of Iberia. After the capitulation of Cadiz in 206 BC Carthaginian power in the peninsula was at an end and Rome could begin to absorb the more civilized south-east into the structure of the nascent empire, using this foothold as a base from which, gradually, to take control of the rest of the peninsula. The exploitation of the conquered territories and the military input needed to expand the frontiers created a constant to-ing and fro-ing between Italy and Iberia which relied heavily on the land route across southern Gaul from the Alps to the Pyrenees. Gradually these lands (now Provence and Languedoc) became used to the Roman presence and close economic ties developed. This is most obviously demonstrated by the increasing quantities of Italic amphorae on southern Gaulish sites – the new markets providing a ready dumping ground for the surplus wine produced on the large estates of Roman Italy.

The eastern arm of the land route around the Maritime Alps was not altogether safe. Hill tribes took delight in raiding Roman baggage trains and terrorizing the coastal cities, and Roman troops had constantly to be sent to drive them back. Eventually, by 120 BC, the situation had so deteriorated that the army stayed and thus a new province – that of Transalpina – was formed. Within a few years, probably in 118 BC, the citizen colony of Narbo Martius (now Narbonne) was founded close to a native settlement which controlled the route westwards from the Mediterranean along the valley of the Aude and via the Carcassonne Gap to the Garonne and Gironde and thence to the Atlantic. With the newly founded colonia at Narbo and the ancient city of Massilia, which commanded the Rhône route northwards into the heart of western Europe, under Roman control, the two natural corridors from the west Mediterranean into barbarian Europe were firmly in Roman hands.

The period from *c*. 120–60 BC saw the consolidation and expansion of Transalpina and its exploitation by Roman entrepreneurs. More to the point, the new province provided a stable base from which Roman traders could penetrate the social systems of the barbarian tribes. Writers like Diodorus Siculus were quite explicit about what was happening. The Gaulish love of wine for use in cycles of feasting and gift-giving created a demand which was willingly satisfied by Italian entrepreneurs eager to find a market for their surplus. Thus

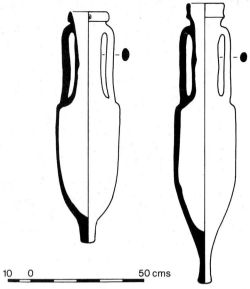

10 0   50 cms

46 *Wine amphorae from Roman states in eastern Italy. Left: Dressel type 1A dating to the late second and early first century* BC. *Right: Dressel type 1B of the late first century* BC.

wine flowed in quantity into barbarian Gaul in return for slaves and, no doubt, other commodities such as metals, furs and foodstuffs. The extent of these early exchange systems is vividly demonstrated by the distribution of the distinctive Roman wine amphorae of Dressel type 1A (**46**).

Much of the transfer of wine would have been enacted in the native oppida close to the frontier of Roman territory and once in native hands it would have been consumed in feasts or distributed in cycles of reciprocal exchange. But by other more complex systems cargoes of amphorae passed up the major rivers and along the Atlantic sea-ways. A glance at the map (**47**) shows that surprising amounts were reaching Brittany, particularly the south coast, and a trail can be traced northwards, via Guernsey, to the central southern British ports at Hengistbury and in Poole Harbour.

The distribution of these Dressel 1A amphorae gives a new visibility to the by now ancient Atlantic exchange routes but the presence of amphorae cannot be taken to imply

47 *The distribution of the two types of Dressel 1 amphorae suggesting a changing emphasis in trade patterns some time about the middle of the first century* BC.

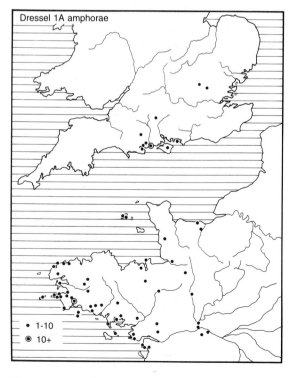

Dressel 1A amphorae

• 1-10
⊙ 10+

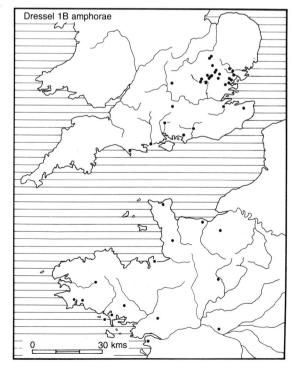

Dressel 1B amphorae

0   30 kms

that Italian shippers were now regularly plying the Atlantic sea-ways. All it need mean is that a new commodity – Mediterranean wine – was now available to add to the goods which were traditionally manipulated in the exchange networks. However that there was a real interest among Roman entrepreneurs in the potential of the Atlantic system cannot be doubted. Indeed it is recorded that Publius Crassus explored the routes himself some time about 100 BC so that he could bring back information for the benefit of Roman merchants. Writing about the period at the end of the first century BC the Greek geographer Strabo lists as the principal exports of Britain, 'grain, cattle, gold, silver and iron... also hides, and slaves and dogs that are by nature suited to the purposes of the chase'. The list is fascinating in that it emphasized the two classes of commodity that the consumer society of the Roman world was most in need of – raw materials and manpower. But it is also interesting that the traditional export of Britain – tin – is not mentioned. There could be many explanations for this omission but, taken at its face value, it could mean that British tin was no longer required, since the metal was now readily available to the Romans from newly acquired territories in north-western Iberia. This may explain why the focus of the trade route at this time was not the south-western peninsula but the harbours of the Solent coast which were more centrally placed for acquiring the full range of commodities the Roman consumers required.

On present evidence the site of Hengistbury Head, overlooking the sheltered anchorage of Christchurch Harbour, seems to have been the principal entrepôt in the early first century BC (**colour plates 10–11**). The headland was admirably sited: it was easily visible from the sea and commanded a quiet bay into which flowed the two major rivers, the Stour and the Avon, which provided easy access to the hinterland. It was also a source of high-quality iron ore (**48**).

A range of exotic imports reached the site from along the Atlantic sea-ways. Large num-

48 *Hengistbury Head, Dorset protecting the sheltered anchorage of Christchurch Bay into which flow the Wessex rivers of the Avon and the Stour. The Iron Age harbour settlement lies on the north (protected) shore of the headland.*

bers of Dressel 1A amphorae dominate the archaeological record, but no less interesting are lumps of unworked purple and yellow glass and the seeds of figs, which together give some idea of the range of high-value/low-bulk commodities which had now entered the exchange systems. The assemblage also contains considerable quantitites of pottery made in Armorica (**49**, **50**) which shows the close links between the two sides of the Channel in this period. Hengistbury served as a centre where a range of British commodities was collected – bronze, silver, gold, salt, shale for bracelets, and corn are all attested, but of the slaves and hunting dogs there is no archaeological trace.

49 *Wheel-made pottery manufactured in Armorica and imported into central southern Britain in the early first century BC.*

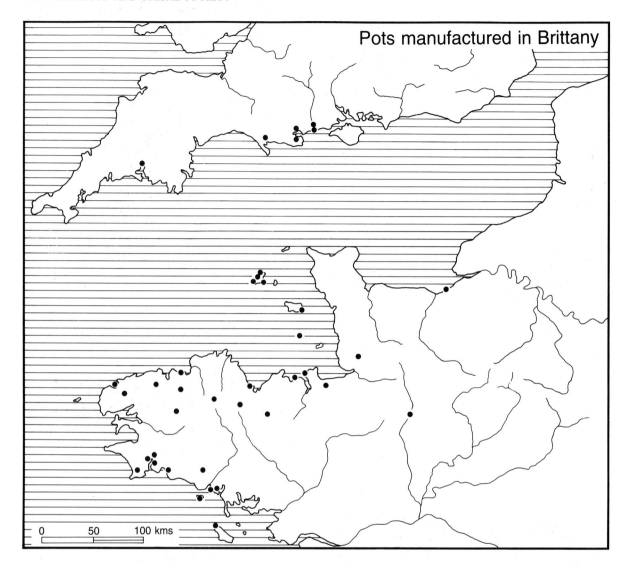

50 *The distribution of Armorican vessels of the type shown in fig.* **49**.

The concentration of such a range of commodities at Hengistbury in this period strongly suggests the intensification of trade some time about or just before 100 BC and very probably the development of fresh channels of contact. It seems highly likely that this phenomenon can be directly related to the much broader pattern of intensified trade, which resulted from the rapid development of the Gaulish market by Roman entrepreneurs in the decades following the establishment of Transalpina in *c.* 120 BC. The exact nature of the settlement at Hengistbury is difficult to demonstrate but from the evidence available it could well have been a specialist trading establishment – a port-of-trade. The very high percentages of Armorican pottery recovered and the presence of Armorican coins from a number of tribes, in particular the Coriosolites of the Côte d'Armor, could imply the presence, for extended periods, of Breton traders who served as the middle men working this arm of the network (**51**, **52**, **53**).

While the western axis of contact introduced an entirely new range of luxury goods into the exchange systems of the central southern region,

51 *Coin of the Coriosolites who originally lived in Armorica, principally in the département of Côtes d'Armor. Many coins of this type have been found in southern Britain suggesting that the tribe may have been involved in cross-Channel trade.*

the south-east continued to remain in close contact with adjacent areas of northern Gaul. This becomes archaeologically more visible because gold coins were now being minted by the Gallo-Belgic tribes for use in gift exchange systems and these found their way into Britain.

52 *Coin of the British king Cunobelinus with a clear representation of a ship on the reverse. Ships of this kind were probably involved in cross-Channel trade.*

53 *Iron anchor and chain found at Bulbury, Dorset. Iron anchors like this were mentioned by Caesar as typical of those used on Breton ships.*

The concentrations of the earliest groups (Gallo-Belgic A, B and C), minted *c.* 130–80 BC, are concentrated in the territories fringing the Thames estuary, especially in Kent, thus clearly distinguishing the tribes of Britain who maintained close political relationships with the Continent at this time. This pattern seems to have closely reflected that of the earlier periods (**54**, **55**).

It is to this second to first century BC period that the problem of the 'Belgic invasion' belongs. As we have mentioned above (p. 19), Caesar, writing in the middle of the first century BC, referred in passing to an incursion of Belgae into Britain at some unspecified time in the past. While it has usually been argued that the

54 *A Gallo-Belgic A coin of a type minted in north Gaul and imported in considerable numbers to Britain early in the first century BC.*

ing southern Britain closely to the Continent in the period *c.* 150–55 BC: the Atlantic system, now greatly intensified by the impact of Roman entrepreneurial demands and with its focus less 'western' than in the previous period; the possibility of a small intrusive group of 'invaders' from the Belgic region north of the Seine into Hampshire; and the maintenance of close socio-political links between the tribes of Kent and Essex and their Gallo-Belgic neighbours. This was the situation in the middle of the first century when Julius Caesar briefly turned his attention to the Britons.

The campaigns of Julius Caesar

In 58 BC, for a variety of complex political, economic and personal reasons, Julius Caesar began to bring the vast expanse of Gaul, as far north as the Rhine, under Roman control. In 55 BC, partly from curiosity, partly to impress his home audience but also to stem the assistance which the Gauls were receiving from Britain, Caesar decided to lead an expeditionary force of two legions with supporting cavalry to Britain. The campaign was far from being a success and after a series of indecisive engagements Caesar withdrew to Gaul, taking British hostages to guarantee the treaties he had managed to conclude.

The next year he returned with a far more substantial force of five legions and 2000 cavalry transported in over 800 ships. The size of such an armada can hardly have failed to have impressed the British opposition gathered on the coast of Kent. The landing and the advance westwards along the ridgeway to a convenient crossing place of the Thames and then northwards into the wilds of Essex was frequently and strongly opposed by native forces which at one time included 4000 war chariots. War leaders were elected and disparate tribal groups worked together to oppose the invaders but

invaders settled in Kent and the Thames valley region and that the Gallo-Belgic coins were associated with the incoming, this now seems less likely, and a case can be made out for a limited (but archaeologically invisible) incursion into the east Solent region penetrating Hampshire. The strongest evidence for this is that under the early Roman reorganization of the province this area of Hampshire, with Winchester as its centre, was known as the canton of the Belgae.

Standing back from the detail we can, then, distinguish three different systems at work link-

55 *Distribution of Gallo-Belgic A and C coins in Britain reflecting close links between south-east Britain and northern Gaul in the early first century BC.*

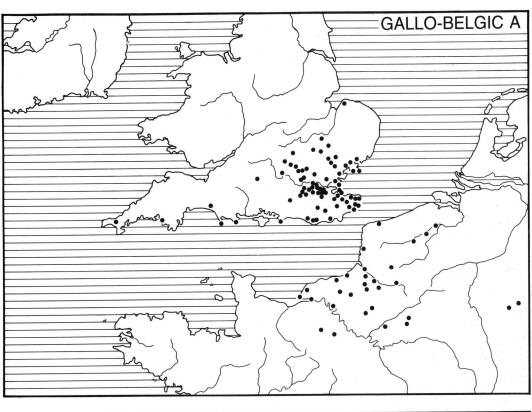

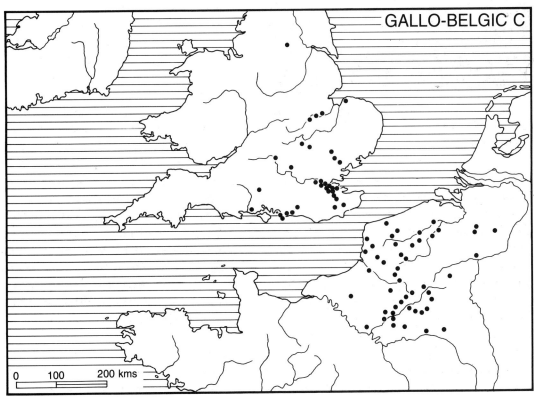

Roman order prevailed over native exuberance and eventually Caesar could depart in good order, having negotiated a series of treaty relationships with tribal elites. The extent of his political success can be measured by the fact that for several decades afterwards Rome could believe that the more civilized parts of Britain were subservient to its will.

After Caesar

The events of 55 and 54 BC introduced an entirely new force – the patronage of Rome – into the already fluid situation in Britain. Those native tribes who were prepared to admit allegiance to Rome could use the threat of Roman intervention to bolster their own power. More directly to the point, the natives of the south-east were now able to develop trading relationships with their traditional partners in Gaul who, because they were now under Roman authority, became the middlemen in rapidly developing networks linked closely to

56 *A considerable similarity in culture existed on both sides of the Channel after Caesar's campaigns. The South Belgic culture continued after the Roman conquest of Gaul. The Aylesford-Swarling culture developed in parallel in Britain, which was still, at this time, free from direct Roman rule.*

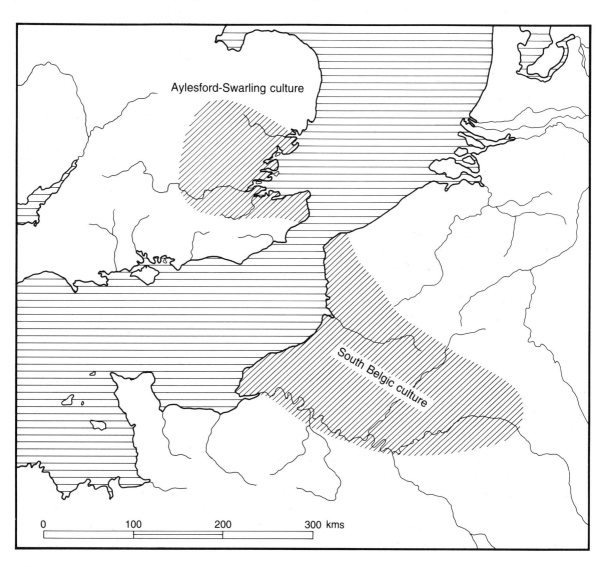

Aylesford-Swarling culture

South Belgic culture

0   100   200   300 kms

the Mediterranean economy. In other words, whereas before Caesar's intervention interchanges between communities on the two sides of the Channel were essentially in the form of gift exchanges between elites, the proximity of the Roman consumer market created the conditions for a new style of commercial trade to develop. Thus the communities of south-eastern Britain became part of a complex network of trading systems extending from the Ouse to the Moselle.

The development of this new eastern axis of trade and exchange coincided with the decline in the old Atlantic routes. This is most dramatically demonstrated by comparing the distribution of Dressel 1A amphorae, the majority of which will have reached Britain before Caesar, with the Dressel 1B type which are largely post-Caesarian (**47**). The conclusion is inescapable – most of the Italian wine which arrived in Britain after the middle of the first century BC must have been consumed by the tribal aristocracies of the south-east.

In the period *c.* 50 BC–AD 43 the communities of Kent, Essex and Hertfordshire developed a culture closely comparable to that of their Continental neighbours. In Britain it is usually referred to as the **Aylesford-Swarling culture** after two Kentish cemetery sites: in Gaul we may call it the **Southern Belgic culture** (**56**). In both areas elegant wheel-turned pottery came commonly into use and cremation, usually in cemeteries, became the normal burial rite.

The burials reflect the ordered nature of society. The great majority were simple cremations placed in urns with few other grave goods. Higher up the social scale we find more elaborate burials with the ashes placed in bronze-bound wooden buckets accompanied by vessels associated with wine drinking, and sometimes with amphorae or items of hearth furniture. The grave assemblages from Aylesford in Kent and Baldock in Hertfordshire are examples of this type (**57**). More elaborate still are the grave chambers of Welwyn type where

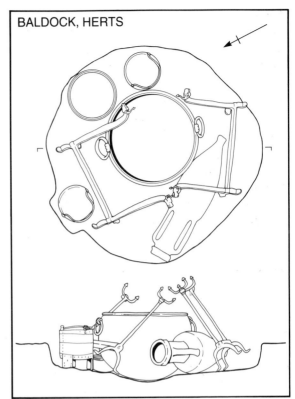

BALDOCK, HERTS

AYLESFORD, KENT

57 *Two richly furnished graves of the Aylesford-Swarling culture.*

the cremated remains are placed in a pit together with an array of goods associated with feasting, as well as the personal equipment of the dead person and other items such as gaming sets (**58**). At the top of the hierarchy were what can reasonably be regarded as kingly burials.

58 *The burial chamber of a chieftain's burial found at Welwyn, Hertfordshire, equipped with everything he would want in the afterlife.*

One, found at Lexden, Colchester, was buried in a pit beneath a barrow 30m (*c.* 100ft) in diameter, with a number of imported luxury goods including several bronze animal attachments, probably from furniture, and a suit of iron chain mail fitted with bronze buckles and hinges and ornamented with silver studs. Other silver attachments included a medallion of the head of the Emperor Augustus (27 BC–AD 14). Fragments of gold fabric were also recovered. In addition the dead aristocrat was provided with at least six Dressel 1B amphorae and more than 12 amphorae of Dressel 2–4 type. Most of the items had been broken up or partly cremated on the funeral pyre before interment.

The Lexden burial probably took place *c.* 15–10 BC but the same tradition, of destroying the grave goods before the grave pit was refilled, has also been recorded at two very rich burials dating to the mid-first century AD, one from Colchester and the other from Folly Lane on the outskirts of Verulamium (St Albans). Although 60 or more years apart in date, the Lexden rites are very similar to those practised at Verulamium and Colchester, where it seems the bodies were laid in state surrounded by

offerings for some time before they were cremated and the grave goods that surrounded the pyre were ritually destroyed. Judging by the quality of the equipment buried with the dead these burials must have been of individuals at, or close to, the top of the social pyramid.

Rich burials were far from evenly distributed in Britain and Gaul in the post-Caesarian period. In Britain there are two principal clusters, one spanning the Chiltern ridge, the other close to the Essex coast, while in northern Gaul one group is found in the Aisne valley in the vicinity of Soisson, the other on the Moselle around Trier. The two Continental groups can most easily be explained by the fact that both lie close to major routes, which in the Augustan period were formalized with roads leading northwards from the hub of the new road network at Lyons, one to Cologne on the Rhine frontier, the other to the Channel port of Boulogne. In both cases the native hierarchies, and their systems of elite display, clearly survived Caesar's invasion and continued for up to half a century afterwards.

The parallel development in Britain flourished without the direct benefits of Romanization but was evidently an integral part of the trade network which brought Italian luxury goods to the courts of the British nobility, while allowing the desirable commodities of Britain to pass into the Roman system. Those communities who were sited at important points on main routes, controlling the ways across the Chilterns or the approaches to the Essex ports, were clearly in a position to exploit the flow of commodities for their own benefit and it is hardly surprising that it was in these two regions that the rich burials clustered.

The system which developed after Caesar's conquest of Gaul was very different from that which had preceded it. Whereas before the processes of exchange had been embedded within the native economies, now the close proximity of Rome just across the Channel was fast introducing a market system which would eventually lead to goods being bought and sold for currency. It is doubtful if a full market system had developed in Britain much before the end of the first century AD, decades after the invasion, but the inexorable move towards that state was well underway in the south-east in the second half of the first century BC.

From hillforts to oppida

It is during the first century BC that a significant change in settlement can begin to be detected in the south-east of Britain. The most dramatic aspect was the widespread abandonment of hillforts during this period. The exact chronology of this 'event' is difficult to establish but, wherever excavations have been on a large enough scale to assess the occupation of forts quantitatively, it is clear that the intensity of occupation diminished rapidly in the first century BC and probably during the first half of that century. Not all hillforts were totally abandoned. At Danebury, for example, the sanctuaries seem to have continued to be visited and at Bury Hill a settlement developed outside the old hillfort gate in the early first century AD. Elsewhere, for example at Maiden Castle, there is some evidence to suggest that occupation continued longer, while at Oldbury, in Kent, an old hillfort seems to have been brought back into defensive use. The picture, therefore, is complicated and the later reuse of sites may have obscured the true trajectory of occupation, especially in the case of sites which have been studied only in small-scale excavations. Yet the overriding impression is that by the early decades of the first century BC the days of the hillfort were over – the system which had begun in the sixth century BC had now, in the south-east of Britain, run full circle.

If this dating is accepted then the socio-economic change which it must reflect was initiated in the period before Caesar's conquests in Gaul, and therefore was the result either of a directional change inherent in the system itself or of the 'bow wave effect' caused by the Romanization of the exchange systems through Gaul, following the creation of the province of Transalpina. But since there is seldom only a single motive force for social change it may well be that the impact of the new trading networks simply acted as a catalyst to changes already underway.

The abandonment of hillforts, which served as central places in the old Middle Iron Age system, seems to be matched by the development of a new type of defended site which we can call the **enclosed oppidum**. Characteristically these sites have one or more defensive earthwork but frequently occupy locations close to river crossings, the rivers themselves providing part of the boundary. The best known of these enclosed oppida are Dyke Hills (Oxon), Salmonsbury (Glos.), Wheathampstead (Herts.) and probably Winchester (Hants.). Each controls a major river crossing. Others of similar character sit close to major land routes, the better known being the three Kentish oppida of Quarry Wood (Loose), Oldbury and Bigbury. Excavations at the sites of enclosed oppida have been minimal but where evidence is available they can be shown to date to the first century BC.

The one site in this group where a thorough programme of research excavations has begun is the native settlement of Calleva (Silchester in Hampshire) which lies beneath the later Roman town. Here it has been possible to demonstrate an initial phase beginning in the mid-first century BC, represented by pits, gullies and other signs of settlement, giving way, c. 20 BC, to a more formalized layout with roads flanking rectangular timber buildings (**59**). The finds, which include imported pottery and metalwork as well as coins, demonstrate the widely flung contacts of the settlement and its increasingly complex organization. In size, location and economic status it is markedly different from the developed hillforts and it clearly lies at the beginning of a process of urban development. Within a century, it was to become the principal Roman town in the reorganized canton of the Atrebates.

There are many questions surrounding these

59 *The Late Iron Age oppidum of Calleva (Silchester) underlies the later Roman settlement. Excavations have exposed evidence of a regular layout of roads, fenced enclosures and timber buildings.*

early enclosed oppida. Some, like Dyke Hills, Silchester and Ilchester, seem to have continued in use until Roman towns were established on, or very close to, their sites. Others like Bigbury and Wheathampstead were probably abandoned as the focus of settlement moved, at Bigbury some 3km (2 miles) to the valley-side site beneath Canterbury and at Wheathampstead 9km (6 miles) to the valley of the Ver, where the Roman town of Verulamium was to develop. Others, like Salmonsbury and Loose, seem to have been abandoned altogether before the conquest. It is a complex picture which reflects the rapid changes underway in the first century BC and early first century AD.

Towards the end of this time a few locations developed a highly complex system of linear earthworks defining vast tracts of land – these have been called **territorial oppida**. At Calleva it is probable that the linear earthworks developed from the earlier enclosed oppidum,

but elsewhere, at Verulamium, Camulodunum (Colchester) and Noviomagus (Chichester/Selsey) no earlier nucleus has been identified. The most fully studied system are the entrenchments of Camulodunum which cover a territory of some 16sq km (6.25sq miles) (**60**). Within the confines of the more widely flung dykes distinct functional areas have been identified – a settlement at Sheepen, possibly a sanctuary at Gosbecks Farm, and several cemeteries including the kingly burial at Lexden. The dykes of Noviomagus are even more extensive and may have been laid out to include the whole of the Selsey peninsula. Here again settlement areas, cemeteries and a possible mint site are found at widely scattered locations within the area defined by the system.

While it must be admitted that the evidence so far available for these territorial oppida is grossly incomplete, it gives the distinct impression that a varied range of activities was undertaken at widely dispersed locations. This kind of system is very different from the usual model which assumes that all the urban functions were concentrated at one small focus, as in the case of Greek or Roman towns.

There can be little reasonable doubt that the enclosed oppida and territorial oppida of the Late Iron Age represent the emergence of an urban system. At many of these sites coins were minted with mint marks giving the name of the centre – *Calle* (Calleva), *Camulo* (Camulodunum) and *Ver* (Verulamium) – and some, as we have seen, were centres for royal burial. But the most impressive evidence for their importance is that so many were developed by the Roman authorities as the urban centres of large administrative regions. The Romans had simply accepted the reality of the political and economic geography of the south-east.

60 *The Late Iron Age oppidum of Camulodunum (Colchester) spread across a considerable territory and was delimited by a complex of banks and ditches of defensive proportions. A Roman fort, the legionary fortress and the later colonia were established within the dykes.*

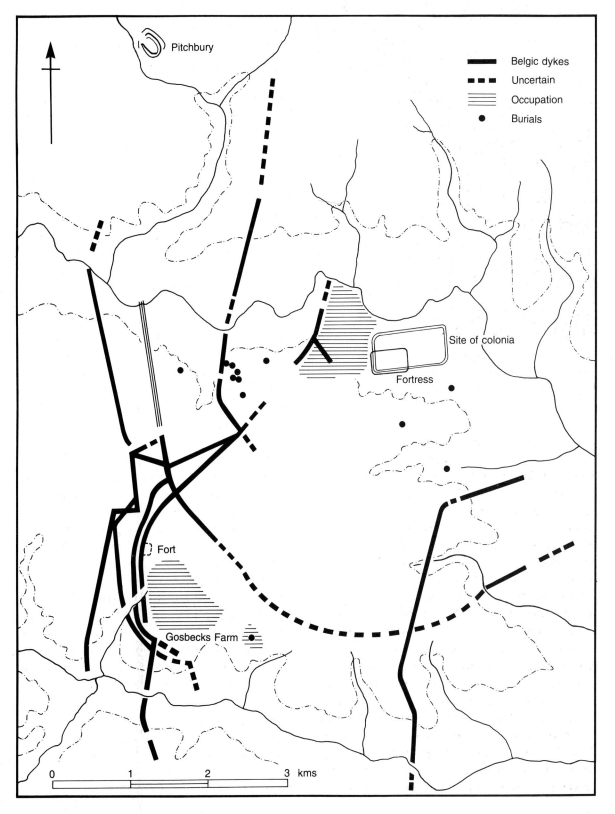

Pitchbury

Belgic dykes
Uncertain
Occupation
Burials

Site of colonia

Fortress

Fort

Gosbecks Farm

0   1   2   3 kms

[handwritten: Caesar's wars ← Influence]

[handwritten: ↳ complex in the value of its different denominations?]

The development of coinage

Coins were first introduced into the British Isles, in large quantities, from Belgic Gaul and Armorica in the period 130–80 BC and soon British tribes began to mint their own. Gallo-Belgic coins continued to arrive in increasingly large quantities up to Caesar's wars. Until this time it is probable that coins were simply used in cycles of gift exchange between elites and between elites and their clients, but after the war British coinage became more complex both in the diversity of its forms and in the value of its different denominations, this latter presumably reflecting the early stages of an emerging market system.

The different coinages of south-eastern Britain provide an invaluable insight into the fast-changing political geography of the last century before the conquest. Beneath the bewildering variety of the different coin types a simple twofold division emerges between a **core zone** and a **peripheral zone**, the divide between them lying roughly along the line from the

61 By the beginning of [...] of Britain had developed [...] territories based largely [...] territories constituted dist[...] 'kingdoms'. Beyond this [...] simply-organized tribes o[...]

[handwritten: the conquest?]

[handwritten: twofold?]

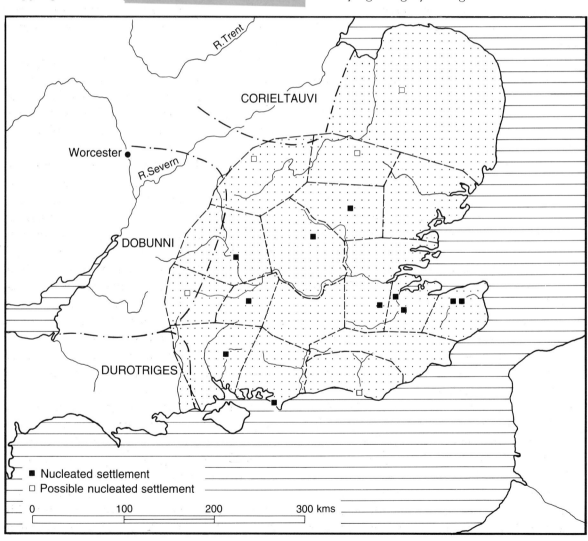

■ Nucleated settlement
□ Possible nucleated settlement

0   100   200   300 kms

Wash to the Solent (**61**). Within the core zone the Thames valley separates two distinct political groupings. The northern polity was dominated throughout by the Catuvellauni and Trinovantes, two tribes at present difficult to distinguish on numismatic evidence, whose territory spread from the Essex coast to the Ouse valley. To the north, isolated in East Anglia were the Iceni who appear to have been politically closely related to the Catuvellauni. South of the Thames the dominant group were the Atrebates, a tribe whose primary focus was Calleva. They seem to have comprised a series of indigenous tribes, possibly with some intrusive Belgic element, given initial coherence by Commius, a Gallo-Belgic leader who fled to Britain in the aftermath of Caesar's Gallic campaigns.

The coin evidence would seem to suggest that Kent was, throughout, a disputed territory and the general picture to emerge is of the gradual ascendancy of the northern polity. This view is given further support by the fact that the northern king, Cunobelinus, is referred to as the 'Great King' of Britain by a contemporary Roman historian. The early course of the invasion in AD 43 is further proof of the importance which the Roman commanders placed on smashing the Catuvellaunian centre at Camulodunum.

Beneath this simple picture it is possible to discern a more complex mosaic of smaller socio-economic units each based on an urban focus. This pattern would seem to be, at least in part, a reflection of the earlier tribal groupings which had emerged during the Middle Iron Age. In other words the early part of the first century BC probably saw the Middle Iron Age tribes and sub-tribes of the south-east each develop a single 'urban' centre in response to the rapidly changing economic scene. After Caesar's campaigns larger confederations were formed in Hampshire and Essex/Hertfordshire and it was the latter group, by virtue of the monopoly which they seemed to have maintained over trade with now-Roman Gaul, who acquired

the greatest power and prestige. By AD 40, the south-east of Britain had become a state in the making under the high king Cunobelinus.

Beyond the western limit of this proto-state, i.e. the core zone, lay three distinct tribal groupings which retained their identity throughout – the Durotriges of Dorset and southern Somerset, the Dobunni of northern Somerset and Gloucestershire and the Corieltauvi of Leicestershire and Lincolnshire. In all three tribal territories large settlements of oppida type emerged during the late first century BC and early first century AD. Among the Durotriges and Dobunni the oppida were generally enclosed but those of the Corieltauvi, sites like Dragonby and Old Sleaford, appear to have been somewhat straggling open settlements.

The western boundary of this peripheral (tribal) zone is not closely defined but it seems to correspond roughly to the axis formed by the rivers Trent, Severn and Exe. Beyond this, to the west, oppida and coin use are unknown – we have entered barbarian territory.

This simple pattern of core–periphery–beyond, seen in its geographic context, marks a dramatic break with the broad settlement geography which had developed throughout the Early and Middle Iron Age. It is, in part, the result of the proximity of the south-east to the Continent but the real motive force behind the reorientation is that generated by the needs of the Roman consumer society. The Roman proximity and its demands caused the social elements of south-eastern Britain to be rearranged into an entirely new pattern, much as a magnet imposes its energy on iron filings which lie within its force field.

The model which emerges, therefore, is a simple one of raw materials and slaves, gleaned from all parts of the British Isles being drawn to the courts of the elite of the northern polity and from there passing across the Channel into the Roman orbit. Such a process would have necessitated very many acts of exchange within the varied social systems still in operation in

Britain. Imagine, for example, the transport of a slave, captured by a Welsh raiding party (**62**), first being given to a member of the Dobunnic aristocracy in a cycle of gift exchange and then changing hands as one of a chained gang in a deal involving gold Dobunnic staters (coins). The slave may then have been acquired for a set of imported pottery vessels by a Catuvellaunian middleman before ending up as the property of an Essex aristocrat, who was accumulating a boatload of servile labour to exchange for an equal number of amphorae of wine just arrived from Gaul. At every point in the system the slave would have attracted added value until he was finally sold in Rome for a price equivalent to six amphorae of quality wine. To the Roman slave dealer this was in the normal run of business, allowing him eventually to acquire a sufficient hoard of wealth to invest in an estate to provide an income for his old age; to the Welsh war lord who captured the slave in a raid it was a way of acquiring an extra cow or two to enhance his prestige.

Beyond the periphery

The pace of development in the core and peripheral zones in the period c. 100 BC–AD 43 was rapid. By the end of this phase of transition most aspects of life would have changed – some of them quite dramatically. In the rest of the British Isles, on the other hand, there is comparatively little evidence for change.

In most parts of south-west Britain and Wales, for example, many of the settlements which had been established in the earlier periods simply continued unchanged, many of them surviving well into the Roman era with little noticeable alteration. Some of those which lay in regions which became more heavily Romanized did experience structural modification: at Mynydd Bychan in Glamorganshire the circular timber houses were rebuilt in stone after the middle of the first century AD while, not far away at Whitton, Romanization took the form first of the replacement of the traditional circular timber house with a rectangu-

lar version at the end of the first century AD. A later rebuilding in masonry converted the establishment to a characteristic 'Roman villa'.

There is less evidence for the continued occupation of hillforts and cliff castles though a few of the forts of north Wales, like the famous Tre'r Ceiri in Caernarvonshire, were in use, if not continuously occupied, well into the Roman period.

In the north-east of Britain there is again ample evidence of continuity, on some sites well into Roman times. At Dalton Parlours on the magnesian limestone of Yorkshire a Middle Iron Age settlement remained in use with little change into the Roman period, when a small masonry villa was eventually constructed. On the other hand at the Cleveland settlement of Thorpe Thewles, where the evidence has been carefully studied, the traditional Middle Iron Age enclosure was replaced in the Late Iron Age by a large open settlement, the inhabitants of which were able to acquire a range of luxury commodities including gold and silver from the south. It seems likely that, by virtue of their location, the people of this eastern lowland region were able to benefit from the intensifying trade systems developing at this time in the south-east.

The upland settlements of Northumberland also underwent a quite noticeable series of

62 *An iron slave chain from the votive deposit of Llyn Cerrig Bach on Anglesey, one of the few surviving indications of the thriving slave trade.*

changes, the most evident of which was the abandonment of strongly defended homestead enclosures for more slightly enclosed farmyards containing one or more stone-walled huts. The locations were now chosen more with an eye to shelter and comfort. The dominant hilltop sites of the earlier period might impress others but they provided little protection from extremes of weather. Over what period this change took place is difficult to say but the new pattern had become widespread by the second century AD.

In the north-west the story is not dissimilar. Here the old broch towers, such a prominent feature of the earlier landscape, seem to have become, visually at least, far less dominant as settlements, like those at Howe and Gurness on Orkney, spread out around them. The chronology of these changes is far from secure but these settlements were probably underway in the first century BC.

The overall impression, then, is that in northern Britain the social pressures which required that status be displayed by the dominance of the residence began to diminish in the first century BC and first century AD. Why this should be is not altogether apparent. It could be that competition became less as pressure on land declined through improved productivity or a slight decline in population. Another possibility is that new forms of social display were adopted, using, perhaps, rare commodities imported from the south. If so little trace of these survives. We must simply admit that, while social change can be detected in these remote regions, the reasons for it remain obscure.

The Roman epilogue

The close links which developed between the tribes of the south-east and the Roman world led inexorably to the invasion of AD 43 – it was yet another example of trade preceding the flag. The initial objective of the invaders seems to have been simply to occupy the core zone which was a comparatively easy task given the complex treaty agreements and other obligations which must have, by then, developed and the fact that the beginnings of an urban system were already in place. The frontier zone, albeit a temporary one, coincided almost exactly with the tribal territories of the peripheral zone – the Durotriges, the Dobunni and the Corieltauvi. The actual frontier was probably the Trent–Severn–Exe line, behind which lay a wide fortified zone with a single military road, the Fosse Way, providing a continuous route from the Humber estuary to Lyme Bay.

This early military system of deployment demonstrated a brilliant understanding of the political geography the civilized south-east was protected and fast on the way to becoming a productive part of the Roman empire, while the tribal territories of the peripheral middle-men were secured together by the Fosse Way. This enabled the military to keep an eye on them and the barbarians beyond, while at the same time taking control of the lucrative trade in slaves and metals which had previously been handled by the tribal elites.

The juddering advance west and north over the three decades following the invasion was interrupted by rebellion, the stiff opposition of Welsh mountain tribes, and upheavals and incompetence in Rome, but by AD 78 much of Britain south of the Forth–Tyne line was under Roman control. The next seven years saw the armies led by Julius Agricola fighting their way through Scotland – a series of campaigns which culminated in a resounding victory over the Highland tribes at Mons Graupius in the foothills overlooking the Moray Firth. After a brief reconnaissance of the Orkney Islands, which may have been undertaken towards the end of the season's campaign, and the subjugation of the inhabitants, Britain could reasonably be regarded as conquered – even though, as events were soon to show, Agricola's gains were transient.

6

Of chiefs and kings

Reconstructing social systems from archaeological evidence is notoriously difficult and there are even those who believe that it cannot or should not be attempted. Such views are defeatist. Indeed it is essential for the archaeologist to look beyond potsherds, post-holes and distribution maps, and to attempt to discover something of the social mechanisms which held together families and allowed them to work in harmony with similar groups to form the larger community. There are many sources of evidence available: the archaeological data; contemporary descriptions by writers like Caesar and Tacitus about the Britons and their Gaulish neighbours whom they were said to resemble closely; the vernacular literature and law tracts of the Welsh and Irish descendants of the native Britons; and the massive anthropological literature based on the painstaking analysis of recently-observed pre-industrial societies. Each source has its strengths and each its inherent dangers. Their value lies in being able to use them all together to constrain and enlighten the models which emerge.

It is worth stressing at the outset that there can be no single correct model for British Iron Age society. In the previous chapters we have shown how varied was the human response to the patchwork of different ecological zones which make up the British Isles and that different areas developed at different rates over time. There would be little value in trying to draw up a single model to attempt to explain the life and values of a Hebridean crofter of the mid-nineteenth century and those of a contemporary merchant family in Liverpool – or for that matter a Hampshire urban craftsman of the thirteenth century and one of the eighteenth century. Differences in location and time are likely to be as significant in the first millennium BC as we can demonstrate they were in the second millennium AD. So what then can reasonably be said?

Caesar's evidence

One possible starting point is Julius Caesar's *Commentaries* on the Gallic Wars. Caesar fought the Gallic tribes over eight campaigning seasons during which he had ample opportunity to observe Gallic society in its various manifestations. From amid the mass of anecdotal, fragmentary and misunderstood 'ethnographic' comment he offers, it is possible to construct a simplified general model. He begins with a fascinating generalization:

> Throughout Gaul there are only two classes of men who are of any account or importance. For the common people are regarded almost as slaves; they never venture to do anything on their own initiative and are never consulted on any subject. Most of them, crushed by debt or heavy taxes or the oppression of more powerful men, pledge themselves to serve the nobles, who exercise over them the

same rights as masters have over slaves. The two privileged classes are the Druids and the Knights.

The distinction between the elite and the servile class is explicit. So too is the web of obligation which bound the lower classes to the elite. Here, presumably, Caesar was observing a system of clientage of the kind that was in operation in early Christian Ireland or in feudal England. In such a system obligations were reciprocal. A man might be expected to provide certain services for his lord but in return he would expect protection.

Elsewhere Caesar makes clear that the size of the entourage of clients that a lord could display was a measure of his social standing. In contemporary Rome the situation was not very different. Here a noble would expect his clients to pay him court in public places such as the baths, so that the size of his following could be observed by his social rivals. The clientage system, then, bound the elite to the lower classes in such a way that both sectors needed each other: they were in a state of equilibrium albeit unstable.

Society also needed mechanisms to maintain harmony among the elite lineages. The practice most commonly used was the giving of daughters as brides – a method adopted widely among the European medieval aristocracy and still to be observed in certain echelons of western society today. Another practice was that of fosterage which involved sending sons to be reared in the houses of others. Fosterage was widespread in early Irish society depicted in the vernacular literature and is implied in a rather obscure passage in which Caesar notes a custom which, he says, was peculiar to the Gauls.

They do not allow their sons to approach them in public until they are youths old enough for military service, and they regard it as disgraceful for a son who is still a boy to stand where his father can see him in a public place.

The picture which Caesar gives of Gaulish society in the middle of the first century BC is one of a world riven by tension and conflict. About this he is quite explicit:

In Gaul, not only every tribe, every canton and every subdivision of a canton, but almost every individual household is divided into rival factions. The leaders of these factions are men thought by their followers to have the greatest prestige.

He goes on to say that similar rivalries divide the tribes. Much the same impression is given by Tacitus writing of Britain a century or so later:

Once they owed obedience to kings; now they are distracted between the warring factions of rival chiefs. Indeed nothing has helped us more in fighting against this very powerful nation than their ability to co-operate. It is but seldom that two or three states unite to repel a common danger; thus, fighting in separate groups, all are conquered.

To what extent this was meant to apply to the whole country or just the south-east is not clear. There is ample evidence of factional differences in the south-east in the half century or so leading up to the invasion. Some time between 10 BC and AD 7 two British leaders, Tincommius and Dubnovellaunus, are recorded to have placed themselves under the protection of Augustus. In AD 39 Adminius, one of Cunobelinus's sons, had fallen out of favour and had fled to the Emperor Gaius to solicit his support and three years later, just before the invasion the last of the Atrebatic rulers, Verica, threw himself on the mercy of the then emperor Claudius. These events, recorded in contemporary texts and on inscriptions, may well be just the tip of the iceberg as the scramble for power intensified. Alternatively they may simply be isolated acts resulting from periods of insecurity as dynasties changed following the death of powerful rulers.

That rivalries among the elite may have been rather more widespread in Britain, in both time and space, is suggested by events among the Brigantes of Yorkshire – a loose confederation of peoples spreading from one side of Britain to the other. To begin with the Brigantes kept out of trouble, pursuing a neutral or pro-Roman policy but in 47–8 'discord' broke out, encouraged perhaps by the Roman advance into north Wales; but, as Tacitus laconically remarks, 'The Brigantes settled down again quietly after the few who had instigated the trouble were killed and the rest pardoned'. In 51 we learn that Queen Cartimandua, who was ruling the Brigantes, turned over a British renegade war leader, Caratacus, to the Romans, presumably to demonstrate the continued loyalty of the client state, but the instability in the confederation became an increasing problem over the next two decades as two different factions emerged, one polarized around the pro-Roman Cartimandua, the other around her husband Venutius who assumed the leadership of the anti-Roman faction. In a fascinating aside Tacitus tells us that 'by cunning stratagems [Cartimandua] captured the brothers and kinsfolk of Venutius', who retaliated by raiding the territory under her control. Eventually the situation deteriorated to such an extent that the Roman army had to move in to extricate Cartimandua, leaving the north in the hands of Venutius. The example illustrates perfectly Tacitus's generalization about Britons being distracted by the warring factions of rival chiefs.

We should, however, remember that we are here dealing with the Britons at the time of their contact with the Romans. The threat or actuality of the Roman military presence must have had a significant impact on society. How far back in time before the mid-first century BC this kind of picture can be projected it is difficult to say, but that some evidence for warfare exists (Chapter 7) suggests that intergroup rivalries were an ever-present reality.

The nature of the tribal hierarchies can dimly be glimpsed from the documentary and archaeological evidence. The situation in Gaul in Caesar's time was in a state of flux as several of the tribes close to the Roman frontier began to adopt a new type of government based on pairs of annually elected magistrates; but ample evidence of the old social system still survived. Among the elite families, one was pre-eminent and provided the chief or king of the tribe to whom all paid allegiance. Some tribal leaders, by virtue of lineage and prowess, exercised wider powers encompassing other tribes. Such a man was Diviciacus, king of the Suessiones in the first half of the first century BC. He was, said Caesar, 'the most powerful ruler in the whole of Gaul, who had control not only over a large area of this region but also of Britain'. Presumably, what Caesar means is that a number of tribes acknowledged his authority by paying tribute. His successor was Galba who 'because of his integrity and good sense had been entrusted by general consent with the supreme command' (Caesar again). This would seem to be an example of a different kind of leadership – that of the war leader elected in time of emergency. Tacitus makes the distinction when, writing of the Germans, he says they 'choose their kings for their noble birth, their commanders for their valour'.

The election of war leaders, while prevalent among the less developed Germanic tribes of the first century AD, may well have largely died out in Gaul, or at least central and southern Gaul by Caesar's time, but the emergency created by Caesar's conquest saw it dramatically revived in the person of Vercingetorix, who rallied the Gauls in opposition to Rome in the great revolt of 52 BC.

A not dissimilar situation had occurred in Britain in 54 BC. As Caesar neatly puts it when describing the British resistance to his advance,

By general agreement the supreme command and direction of the campaign had been given to Cassivellaunus.... Previously [he] had been in a continual state of war with the other tribes, but our arrival had frightened the Britons into appointing him commander-in-chief for the campaign.

Cassivellaunus had, in fact, previously killed a king of the Trinovantes and had driven out his son Mandubracius, who had fled to Caesar in Gaul. Although Cassivellaunus was able to command a huge force, including 4000 chariots, in his opposition to Caesar and to send orders to the four kings of Kent to initiate an attack on the Roman supply base, as soon as it appeared that the Romans were gaining an upper hand the unstable alliance began to fragment. Not surprisingly the Trinovantes were among the first to defect, offering to surrender to Caesar if Mandubracius were returned and the tribe put under Roman protection. In view of these defections and the evident superiority of Roman arms Cassivellaunus was forced to negotiate a peace with Caesar.

Ninety years later, when in AD 43 the Claudian armies attacked, opposition again seems at first to have been united under the command of Caratacus and Togodubnus, the sons of the Catuvellaunian king Cunobelinus who had died a year or two before. When the opposition force was defeated in Kent and Togodubnus was killed, Caratacus fled to the west, using his authority to lead first the Silures of south Wales and later the Ordovices of north Wales against Rome. In AD 51, no doubt in expectation that he could continue to lead an opposition, he moved north to the Brigantes, where Queen Cartimandua turned him over to the Roman authorities. That he had conducted an active anti-Roman campaign for eight years among tribes far from his home is a vivid indication of the extra-tribal power of a war leader. The rebellion of Queen Boudica which broke out in AD 60, engulfing much of south-eastern Britain, is another example of the power which a single charismatic figure could wield in times of crisis.

Tacitus's reference to the Britons *once* being ruled by kings, *now* being distracted between the warring factions of rival chiefs, might be

63 *Gold stater of Verica who claimed to be a son of Commius (COM·F). Verica styles himself REX.*

thought to imply a change in the style of leadership in the recent past but in all probability the words 'king' and 'chief' were being used imprecisely or interchangeably. There were four 'kings' in Kent at the time of Caesar's conquest. The word king – *rex* – is used on various of the early British coinages (**63**), beginning with that of Commius in the second half of the first century BC, and at the time of the invasion of AD 43 Suetonius could describe Cunobelinus as *rex Britannorum*, implying, as we have said, that he wielded authority over a large part of south-eastern Britain. Presumably, therefore, it was a term widely adopted, at least from the first century BC, though it must have encompassed leaders controlling 'kingdoms' of varying sizes.

To what extent 'kingdoms' existed outside the core zone of the south-east is unclear. In the peripheral zone the tribal coinage of the Corieltauvi and Dobunni bear the names of individuals who may well have been 'kings' in the sense that the leaders of the tribes of the core zone were kings, but this is not necessarily so and we may be seeing, at least among the Corieltauvi, elected magistrates or even moneyers putting their names on the coins. Beyond the peripheral zone there is little evidence of how the elite viewed themselves or were seen by the Romans. Cartimandua of the Brigantes was referred to as a 'queen' but in the description of the battle of Mons Graupius in AD 84 Tacitus refers to the war leader Calgacus as 'one of the many leaders, a man of outstanding valour and nobility'. The avoidance of the word king may well have been deliberate but whether this means that there were no kings among these northern tribes or simply that Calgacus was a war leader elected for the occasion, in the sense we have previously discussed, it is impossible to say.

Cemetery evidence

The recognition of the nobility in the archaeological record rests largely upon the interpretation of cemetery evidence which, in the British Isles, in contrast to the Continent, is partial in the extreme. Over much of the country for most of the time the dead were disposed of in a way which has left little or no archaeological trace (below, pp. 108–11). The exceptions to this generalization are the cemeteries of the Arras culture of Yorkshire, the cremations of the Aylesford-Swarling culture of the south-east and the inhumations found scattered throughout the south-west.

The Arras culture burials of the Yorkshire Wolds allow a clear status differentiation to be made between the few high-status burials

accompanied by two-wheeled vehicles and the rest of the burials, which for the most part were without elaborate grave goods except for brooches and joints of pork. The majority of the elite burials were, to judge from the swords which were present, those of male warriors, but one of the vehicle burials found at Wetwang Slack was accompanied by a mirror, a decorated bronze box, and a gold and iron pin enlivened with coral and was without weapons. If, as seems likely, this was the interment of a female, then the vehicle burial ritual was related to status rather than gender.

From the end of the second century BC a few inhumations with grave goods are found in various parts of the British Isles. Both male and female graves can be recognized. The male graves are usually accompanied with weapons, swords, shields and sometimes spears. A few have been found in the Arras culture region, e.g. at North Grimston; others occur more sporadically in the south, in Hampshire (Owslebury), Dorset (Whitcombe) and the Isle of Wight (St Lawrence) (**64**). Their female counterparts usually have mirrors (**65**) and sometimes bronze bowls or beads. The earliest of these, dating to the fourth century, were found at Arras; later examples are known from as far afield as Colchester, Birdlip (Glos.), Mount Batten (Devon) and Trelan Bahow (Cornwall).

The evidence for rich burials, outside the Late Iron Age cremating region of the south-east, is not extensive but it does show that the most elaborate high-status burials, with vehicles, occurred early, in the fifth–third centuries, in a very restricted area of south Yorkshire after which the rite became geographically more widespread but without the accompanying vehicle. In the south-east, as we have seen above, cremation burials became the norm after the middle of the first century. Over and above the normal run of burials three quite distinct groups can be defined – the bucket burials of Aylesford type, the amphora burials of Welwyn type and the 'kingly' burials of

Owslebury,Hants

Whitcombe,Dorset

1.Bronze fibula
2.Circular belthook
3.Iron spearhead
4.Circular lump of chalk
5.Iron sword
6.Iron tool
7.Iron hammer
8.Broken bronze object

1.Iron spearhead,ferrula and bronze strip
2.Iron sword
3.Bronze rings from sword belt
4.Silvered bronze belthook
5.Bronze shield boss

0   100   200 cms

64 *Two warrior burials from southern Britain. Both men were equipped with a full set of weapons.*

Lexden type, representing different echelons in the social hierarchy.

It would be quite inappropriate to attempt to interpret this scattered burial evidence in social terms except at a very simple level. In the south Yorkshire region and in the south-east it is, however, clear that elites were distinguished by characteristic burial practices and that several social strata can be identified. It is also interesting to note that women were offered rites of equal status to men, a point to which we shall return below. It may be that some of the richer burials were those of chief-tains or kings but such a correlation is difficult to prove. It is also tempting to see the sword burials as those of warriors. What must, how-ever, be stressed is that over much of the country, except south Yorkshire, the burials that survive represent a minority rite, the vast majority of the dead having been disposed of in some other way. It could be, for example, that kings were cremated and their ashes, together with their equipment, being thrown into rivers. This could explain the amount of elaborate warrior gear recovered from rivers and dating to throughout the first millennium; but the same evidence could have resulted from other types of ritual deposition. Thus, the nature of the archaeological evidence is such

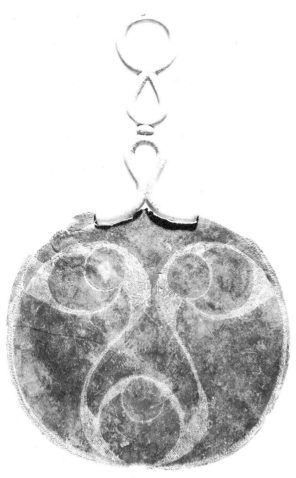

65 *Bronze mirror from Aston, Hertfordshire. It is tempting to see in the curvilinear design a face staring out. (Compare with* **colour plate 5***.)*

that we are unlikely ever to be able to reconstruct social systems from the burial data alone.

The position of women

We have already noted that among the Arras vehicle burials there is evidence to show that females were accorded the same rite as males and that the later 'mirror' burials found more widely throughout the country were probably the female counterparts to the 'sword' burials. This suggests that, in some communities at least, the status of females may have equalled that of men at least from the fifth century BC.

The classical sources for the first century AD provide clear evidence that women could play leading roles in Late Iron Age society. Queen Cartimandua of the Brigantes was able to rival the authority of her estranged husband Venutius, albeit with Roman support, while Queen Boudica, widow of the Icenian king Prasutagus, had the authority, and the personality, to lead many of the tribes of south-eastern Britain in open revolt against the occupying Romans. There is no reason at all to suppose that these two women were exceptional in British Iron Age society.

There are some hints in the contemporary literature about the status of women generally in society. Writing of Gaulish marriage arrangements Caesar records that

> when a man marries, he contributes from his own property an amount calculated to match whatever he has received from his wife as her dowry. A joint account is kept of all this property and the profits from it are set aside. Whichever of the two outlives the other gets both shares together with the profits that have accumulated.

Such an arrangement is neatly matched in the Irish epic the *Táin Bo Cuailnge* which begins with the king and queen, Ailill and Medb, in bed together in the fort of Cruachain in Connacht discussing the wealth each has brought to the marriage. As the conversation becomes more competitive the possessions of each are paraded and matched equally until the last when Medb realizes that she has no bull as great as Ailill's Finnbennach – the White Horned. Her pride devastated, she determines to acquire the great Brown Bull of Cuailnge and thus the scene for the cattle raid is set.

In Gaul, males and females did not have equal rights. Husbands, Caesar writes, had power of life and death over their wives and children and this power was exercised by the husband's kin if he had died in suspicious circumstances. Widows could then be examined under torture and if found guilty would be burnt to death.

It is impossible to say whether or not the Gaulish model applied in Britain. Caesar's only comment on the position of women in the south-east of the country is difficult to interpret in conventional social terms:

> Wives are shared between groups of ten or twelve men, especially between brothers and between fathers and sons; but the children of such unions are counted as belonging to the man with whom the woman first cohabited.

He gives no indication how widespread this practice was or if it was restricted to any particular social class. Indeed it remains a possibility that he misinterpreted what was reported to him.

That there may have been social, regional or chronological differences is shown by the case of Cartimandua, who, after breaking with her husband, consorted with his armour bearer. This is a particularly informative incident for by doing so she was deliberately insulting him and at the same time weakening his power by removing from his entourage a trained fighting companion. The armour bearer in this case was probably equivalent to the squire who served the medieval knight.

Skilled men

Alongside the nobility there would have been a wide range of skilled men, each occupying a distinct place in the social hierarchy. Caesar mentions specifically only the Druids who were held in the highest esteem and exercised powers transcending those of the nobility. Below them were men with other skills who probably served in the retinues of the elite. Several classical writers refer to the bards, among whose tasks were to sing the praises of their masters and to demean his opponents by satirizing them – the destructive power of their words was devastating. The classical writer Athenaeus mentions a sumptuous party put on by the wealthy Gaulish chieftain Lovernius at which a bard arrived too late. Not to be outdone he ran behind the chief's chariot singing his praises 'in a hymn extolling his greatness and lamenting his own lot for having arrived late'. Lovernius, suitably

flattered, threw the bard a bag of gold as he ran. The quick-thinking bard thereupon sang another song in his honour 'saying that the wheel-tracks made by the chariot...bore golden benefits for men'. A mixture of sly wit and sycophancy paid dividends in the Gaulish world.

Among the other much sought after skills were those of the craftsmen, particularly workers in metal – men capable of making the flashy fittings for horse tackle, the elaborate sword sheaths and bronze shield fittings or coverings, the finely engraved mirrors and the cumbersome gold torcs found in such profusion in East Anglia – indeed all the flamboyant gear necessary for the aristocracy to express itself.

An insight into the reality of such craft activity was provided by a remarkable find, at the Dorset settlement of Gussage All Saints, of a collection of bronze-working debris which had been dumped in a pit (**66**). The collection included triangular crucibles, a billet of tin bronze, bone spatulae for making wax models, a variety of iron punches and chisels for the fine working of metal, and a mass of fragments from clay moulds for making various harness and cart fittings including terret rings, bridles, strap unions and linchpin terminals. The process employed and indeed the pyrotechnic skills required were really quite straightforward. First the required bronze item was modelled in beeswax. The model was then invested with a fine refractory clay leaving a small vent to the wax model. After careful drying the whole was baked during which process the wax melted and was poured away. The second stage involved melting copper alloy in a crucible and pouring it into the void left by the wax. After cooling, the mould would be broken open and the cast bronze item removed for the final stage of cleaning, tooling and polishing.

Very little equipment would be needed for such an activity other than a few basic tools, some refractory clay and a lump of beeswax – things that could easily be carried by the individual craftsman. The copper alloy used

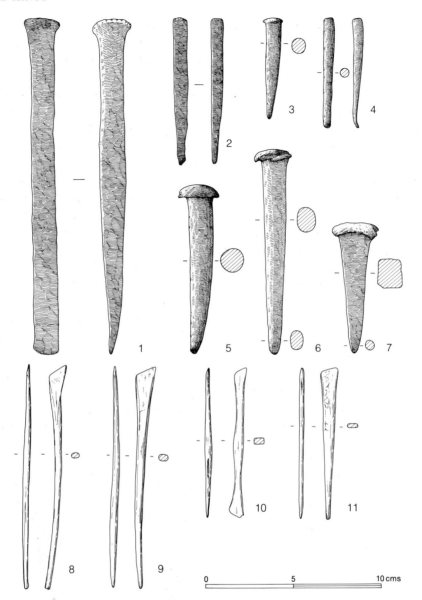

66 *A selection of metalworker's tools from Gussage All Saints, Dorset. The iron implements (1–7) were punches and chisels for bronzeworking; the bone implements (8–11) were spatulae for making wax proformas for the 'lost wax' process of casting.*

might have been provided by the craftsman but it could equally well have come from recycled scrap acquired at the settlement. The billet of metal from Gussage could have been cast from scrap on the spot into a convenient form for handling – it was only 11cm ($4\frac{1}{2}$in.)

long. At Danebury the raw material was carried in the form of filings in a small leather bag.

The Gussage craftsman was involved in a prodigious production. Some 8000 fragments of clay mould were recovered from his operations, representing the manufacture of about 50 sets of bronze horse trappings – an activity which need not have taken more than a few weeks at the very most. Whether or not he was working alone is impossible to say. One interesting possibility is that he was one of a team of men making chariots and the tackle needed to harness the pairs of ponies: the linchpins, which prevented the wheel from slipping off the axle, shows that some of his output was associated with vehicles as well as harnessing. To support such a suggestion the excavator has noted that the animal bones found on the site could reflect some element of horse breeding. One possibility, therefore, is that the lord of Gussage retained in his retinue a team of specialists who could, when necessary, work together to produce trained pony teams and chariots. The output of 20–30 such teams in a short period of time might seem to be rather excessive unless it was a response to an event (let us not forget the 4000 chariots that Cassivellaunus was able to call up to oppose Caesar) or the need to produce prestige gifts for use in a conspicuous cycle of gift exchange.

These speculations do not, however, make clear the exact social position of the Gussage craftsman. Was he a permanent member of the entourage of the resident lord or was he an itinerant who moved from site to site with his tool kit, bag of clay and lump of wax? Both models are equally possible. To take a minimalist view it is worth pointing out that a single craftsman could easily, in the course of a working life, have made all the bronze horse gear known in Wessex. This is not for one moment to suggest that there was only one but to stress the point that there may have been comparatively few skilled bronzesmiths working at any one time.

Bronze casting was only one of the specialist metalworking skills in operation in Britain; another, of much greater prestige, was sheet bronze-work, leading to the production of repoussé decorated and engraved sword sheaths, shields, helmets and pony caps. The sword and shield from the river Witham, the shield bosses from the Thames at Wandsworth and the pony cap from Torrs in Scotland represent the peak of achievement in the third or second century BC (**67**). It is even possible that they were the product of a single craft school. The same possibility can also be raised about

the remarkable collections of gold torcs from eastern England of which the Snettisham and Ipswich hoards provide the prime examples.

In all these cases, craftsmen of immense skill and with easy access to rare raw materials were able to devote themselves to the production of luxury goods for their masters to manipulate, in order to enhance their own prestige. For the elite social system to maintain itself it was essential that men with such skills should have a precisely defined position in society so that they could enjoy the patronage necessary to enable them to practise and to teach.

Regional variation

Most of what has been said so far in this chapter has an anecdotal rather than a systematic character and relates to the later period for which some textual evidence is available. How

67 *The so-called 'Torrs chamfrain' – a curious composite item made by attaching drinking horn terminals to a pony cap (cf. figs* **10**, **11**) *– represents the work of a school of metalworking masters of the third and second centuries. The pieces may have been assembled into a single object more recently.*

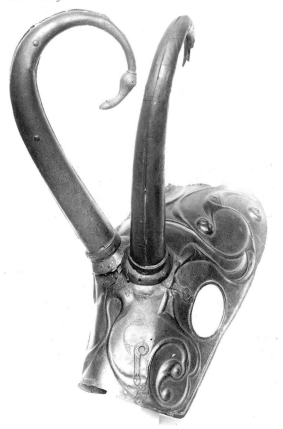

far back in time and over what geographical area this generalized picture of aristocratic society is relevant is harder to say, but to explore the question we must revert to a consideration of the settlement pattern evidence.

There is a certain broad cohesion about the settlement evidence from the west which suggests a degree of similarity over long periods of time and large expanses of territory. The enclosed homestead dominating its immediate landscape is strongly suggestive of small social units little larger than the family or extended family. In several parts of the region, most notably in Cornwall, south-west Wales and Caithness pairs of settlements in fairly close proximity can be distinguished. It is usually impossible to demonstrate any degree of contemporaneity but if, as seems not unreasonable, some at least of these pairs were occupied at the same time, then this is the kind of pattern which would be expected if a system of partable inheritance was in operation with the elder sons moving out of the parental home to live nearby. Such a system was long practised in the west and gives the present Welsh and Breton countryside their distinct characteristics. There is little evidence in these areas of wealth and power accumulating in the hands of an aristocracy or of the communal works which would be expected of a more complex social organization.

In the centre south, as we have seen, the picture is very different. The settlements vary in size and complexity, presumably reflecting social status, and the development of hillforts is indicative of some degree of communal organization, involving the provision of centralized facilities. In some of the more elaborate settlements and the hillforts luxury items, such as elaborate horse gear, are frequently found. This kind of settlement evidence would be consistent with a stratified society comprising an elite class with their entourages and lower social levels of more subservient producers. In such a system the developed hillforts could be seen as the residences of the elite class whose patronage extended to providing leadership,

protection and a range of services for the whole community.

What little is known of the east of Britain in the Middle Iron Age suggests a rather different social system, more akin to that of the North European Plain where the village formed the focal unit. It must be admitted that the evidence is still far from clear. Even in this zone the burials of the Arras culture are sufficient to show that, in one area and for several generations, there existed a society in which warrior prowess was a mark of elite status.

The economic changes which came about in the south-east, as contact intensified with the European mainland, would have caused widespread social changes in the region. The most likely is the gradual amalgamation of the smaller chieftain-dominated groups into larger confederacies. These crystallized into distinct socio-political units which recognized the authority of overlords – the 'kings' who emerge in the numismatic and textual evidence of the last century of freedom. Close examination of the coin evidence allows a complex quasi-history to be created, illustrating the sometimes transient nature of these kingdoms as dynasts competed for control. There is nothing inherently difficult in accepting this generalized picture. By the time of the conquest much of the south-east had come under the expanding authority of the Catuvellaunian/Trinovantian royal house.

What we are witnessing in the south-east in the first century BC and early first century AD is the process of state formation – it was society in a state of flux. For this reason the impression of restless social turmoil commemorated by the classical writers may well be correct but it cannot be assumed to be the norm for Britain as a whole. Beyond the south-east a simpler social structure and a more tranquil pace of life is likely to have persisted. The family occupying the broch on the island of Mousa in the Shetlands in the early decades of the first century AD will have had a very different life style to a family living within the defences of the newly replanned oppidum of Calleva.

7
War mad but not of evil character

The Celts in Europe

The characteristic of the Celtic peoples which most impressed itself upon the consciousness of the classical writers was their ferocity in battle. The Greek geographer Strabo, writing at the end of the first century BC, but making extensive use of earlier sources, offers the much-repeated stereotype:

> The whole race ... is madly fond of war, high spirited and quick to battle, but otherwise straightforward and not of evil character. And so when they are stirred up they assemble in their bands for battle, quite openly and without forethought ... and on whatever pretext you stir them up, you will have them ready to face danger even if they have nothing on their side but their own strength and courage.

Like many racial stereotypes there was just sufficient truth in it to ring true. The Roman world had faced vast armies of 'Celts' from north of the Alps, who swept into the Po valley in the fifth century and later thrust deep into the Italian peninsula destroying parts of Rome itself in 390. It was not until the opening decades of the second century BC that the last of the major confrontations had been fought and the various Celtic tribes occupying the fertile lands between the Appenines and the Alps had been subdued or driven out. The Greeks too knew what it was like to face rampaging Celtic armies for, in 279, huge numbers of barbarian raiders had overrun the eastern coastal routes to reach Delphi. These traumatic episodes will have created in the folk memory a terrifying vision of the northern barbarian – a vision magnified by the retelling – a warning to naughty children.

Yet behind it all was the reality. In 225 BC at Telemon on the west coast of Tuscany the Roman army confronted a massive Celtic force in an engagement made famous by the vivid writing of the Greek historian Polybius. Having described the nakedness of one of the leading barbarian contingents, the Gaesatae, and the fury of the cavalry engagement, in which the Roman consul was beheaded, Polybius goes on to conjure up the terror inspired in the Roman troops by

> the fine order of the Celtic host, and the dreadful din, for there were innumerable horn-blowers [(**68**)] and trumpeters, and as the whole army were shouting their war-cries out there was such a tumult of sound that it seemed [as if] all the country round had got a voice and caught up the cry. Very terrifying too were the gestures of the naked warriors in front, all in the prime of life and finely built men, and all in the leading companies richly adorned with gold torcs and armlets.

After some while the Roman forces gained the advantage and the fury of the Celts turned in upon itself. Some of them

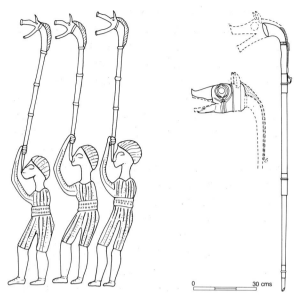

68 *Warriors blowing war trumpets (carnexes), from the Gunderstrup cauldron found in Denmark. Right: actual fragments of war trumpets, the head from Deskford, Banff, the tube from Tattershall Ferry, Lincolnshire.*

in their impotent rage rushed wildly on the enemy and sacrificed their lives, while others, retreating step by step on the ranks of their fellows threw them into disorder by their display of faint-heartedness.

The battle of Telemon provides then the archetype of the Celt at war. As a picture of the marauding warrior groups of the third century BC we need not doubt its accuracy, but times change and different geographies constrain social systems. This point was well made by Strabo who followed his famous 'war mad' description by reminding his reader that in Gaul all were now living in peace under Roman rule, 'but this view of them I take from former times and from the customs which still remain to the present day among the Germans'.

While the Greek and Roman 'ethnographic' descriptions are little more than anecdotes, taken together they do allow us to construct a broad model within which to attempt to interpret the evidence of warfare. Success in battle was the way in which a young man could acquire status. By persuading a number of

fellows to follow him he could demonstrate his powers of leadership and by leading a successful raid he could reward his followers with a share of the booty, thus enhancing his powers of patronage. Success in the one increased chances of success in the other.

The feast seems to have provided the occasion at which status was publicly proclaimed and affirmed. In cutting up the carcass of meat and offering specific cuts, each of which took with it a statement of the status of the recipient, the carver was making a public judgment of the social position of each of the assembled company. It was open to anyone to dispute the assessment. Sometimes the dispute led to combat between two contestants but by the end of the feast the position of everyone had been publicly affirmed. It was on such occasions that aspiring war leaders would announce expeditions and solicit followers (**colour plate 7**).

The raids which followed the ceremonies were against neighbouring tribes. Cattle, women and other plunder gained on such an occasion and distributed among the participants would add to the tribal wealth. In this way boundaries were maintained and often there was a zone of no man's land between competing tribes. In times of peace no doubt raiding ceased and alliances were formed, but warfare was endemic within the social system and in extreme cases could become central to the social trajectory of the tribe. Tacitus, writing of the Germans in the late first century AD, gives a succinct account of such a case. The German, he says,

is not so easily prevailed upon to plough the land and wait patiently for harvest as to challenge a foe and earn wounds for his reward. He thinks it tame and spiritless to accumulate slowly by the sweat of his brow what can be got quickly by the loss of a little blood. . . . The boldest and more warlike men have no regular employment, the care of house, home, and fields being left to the women, old men, and weaklings of the family.

It was, presumably, this kind of situation which prevailed in the Po valley in the fourth and third centuries BC, which provided the stable base from which the Celtic war bands operated crossing the Appenines to range wide throughout the peninsula as freelance raiders or as mercenaries. An exactly similar situation existed in Asia Minor in the third and second centuries when the Celtic tribes, who had settled in the Ankara region, raided the rich cities of the Aegean coast.

While raiding was the normal expression of aggression, opposing forces sometimes met in the open field. On such occasions the two groups confronted each other across an open space and, at first at least, the conflict might be restricted to single combat between matched opponents in full view of the assembled companies. In this way the aggression might be defused but a more all-inclusive mêlée could result. There are interesting indications in the classical sources that in the early conflicts with the Romans in Italy single combat sometimes played a part. Later, however, Roman tactics of all-out battle determined the course of events and by the time of the Gallic Wars there is little detectable difference between the fighting methods of the two sides (**69**).

69 *Coin of Verica depicting a mounted warrior armed with spear, sword and shield.*

Britain: the literary evidence

Sufficient has now been said of first millennium BC warfare in western Europe to provide a context within which to consider the evidence from Britain. An obvious starting point is the situation in 55 and 54 BC when the Roman army confronted the Britons of Kent and Essex for the first time. Caesar's first-hand description of these encounters provides an invaluable record of British fighting methods in the southeast before extensive contact with the Roman world brought about changes.

On the initial landing in 55 BC Caesar describes the British force as comprising foot soldiers, cavalry and chariots, all three of which were regularly used in battle (**colour plate 13**). He was evidently impressed by the chariots, which he appears not to have encountered before in Gaul and gives a full description of the tactics involved.

> First they drive in all directions hurling spears. Generally they succeed in throwing the rank of their opponents into confusion just with the terror caused by their galloping horses and the din of the wheels. They make their way through the squadrons of their own cavalry, then jump down from their chariots and fight on foot. Meanwhile the chariot-drivers withdraw a little way from the fighting and position the chariots in such a way that if their masters are hard pressed by the enemy's numbers, they have an easy means of retreat to their own lines. Thus when they fight they have the mobility of cavalry and the staying power of infantry: and with daily training and practice they have become so efficient that even on steep slopes they can control their horses at full gallop, check and turn them in a moment, run along the pole, stand on the yoke and get back into the chariot with incredible speed.

Caesar was evidently impressed and referred twice more to the devastating tactic of dismounting from the chariots and fighting on foot. The number of chariots was large: at one

70 *Bronze shield from Chertsey, Surrey. Very similar to the shield carried by the horseman in fig.* **69**.

stage Cassivellaunus had 4000 under his command. The Romans found the flexibility of British fighting methods difficult to contend with. The natives never fought in close order but in scattered groups. They kept back numbers of reserves concentrated at intervals, who could cover the retreat of their comrades and provide fresh troops to take over when required. To a Roman, trained in ordered close-formation fighting, all this was very unnerving.

Caesar's description of the fighting techniques of the Britons leaves little doubt that he was facing a warlike people thoroughly experienced in the arts of battle for whom the sword and spear were ever-present (**70**) – this was no group of farmers dragged reluctantly from the fields to drive the invaders from their

shores. The Roman presence provided the native elite with the same opportunity to demonstrate prowess and to acquire booty as did traditional patterns of conflict with neighbouring tribes.

Before tracing these systems of warfare backwards into the truly prehistoric period it is worth briefly taking the story up to the period of the conquest. What stands out with particular clarity is how little native methods of warfare change over the century. During the Claudian invasion the tribes of the south-west resorted to the protection of hillforts which, though admirable against the short-lived fury of local raids, were useless against the siege tactics which Vespasian's troops adopted. More than 20 of these forts were rapidly overcome.

Even more surprising are the archaic methods of warfare used in AD 60 by the Icenian queen, Boudica, at the time of the rebellion against the occupying Romans. When eventually the two armies met the British forces were spread out over a large area, divided into small bands of infantry and cavalry, and their families who had come to watch stood on wagons at the edge of the battlefield. The queen in her chariot was driven about shouting boastful support amid the roar and din of her warriors, designed to intimidate their opponents. The scene, sketched for us by Tacitus, was typical of the setpiece Celtic battles of the distant past. Boudica's use of the chariot is made more interesting by the fact that no other reference is made of them. Perhaps her vehicle was a symbol of traditional leadership, chariots no longer being used in warfare. Alternatively they could still have been so common in Britain that Tacitus's source did not bother specifically to mention them. We do know that they were in active use 17 years previously at the time of the Claudian invasion.

The last great confrontation between the Britons and the Romans was the battle of Mons Graupius, fought in the north of Scotland in AD 84 between the Roman forces commanded by Agricola and Caledonians under the leadership of Calgacus. Here, once more, we see the British chariot in action. Tacitus describes how in the immediate prelude to the battle the flat space between the two confronting armies was taken up by the noisy manœuvrings of the charioteers, no doubt (though he does not say so) carrying the elite so they could show their daring and shout their abuse in full view of their own supporters.

> The fighting began with exchanges of missiles, and the Britons showed both steadiness and skill in parrying our spears with their huge swords or catching them on their own little shields while they themselves rained volleys on us.

Once the troops were fully engaged Roman force of arms began to tell: the cavalry routed the war chariots and the British infantry were cut to pieces in the speed of the Roman advance.

> Whole groups, though they had weapons in their hands, fled before inferior numbers; elsewhere unarmed men deliberately charged to face certain death.

Here Tacitus may be guilty of calling up the stereotype of the unstable Celtic warrior, which we encountered at Telemon 300 years earlier, but perhaps the unruly boastfulness which was required by the long-established social system conditioned such behaviour. As Strabo so succinctly puts it, 'It is this vanity which makes them unbearable in victory and so completely downcast in defeat'.

We need hardly stress that to impose a generalized picture of 'Celtic warfare' gleaned from the fragmentary classical sources on the whole of the British Isles throughout the Iron Age would be a nonsense, and yet we must accept that the inhabitants of Kent and Essex who opposed Caesar in the first century BC were well practised in warfare of a kind noted earlier among the 'Gauls' or 'Celts' of the Continent. To examine how widespread were these systems in the prehistoric Iron Age we must turn to the archaeological evidence.

Weapons and hillforts

In the eighth and seventh centuries BC evidence of warfare is restricted to a study of weapons which occur in plenty. The heavy bronze slashing sword, bronze-headed spears and round shields of leather, sometimes covered in sheet bronze, are found widely scattered across the British Isles, though the items are usually found in hoards or thrown as votive offerings into rivers or lakes rather than in settlement sites. The quality of the items implies that they were made for an elite by schools of specialized craftsmen.

In the seventh and sixth centuries new styles of weapons developed on the Continent and these were quickly adopted and adapted in Britain. It was at this time that horse trappings, which were known earlier, became rather more widespread. On the Continent, in a broad zone stretching from eastern France to Bohemia, the elite began to be distinguished by distinctive burial rites. Some, presumably the minor nobility, were buried with weapons and horse gear while others, the paramounts, were buried with funerary carts. It is tempting to see in this a distinction between chieftains and the more lowly warrior class. The definition of the warrior in the burial ritual is indicative of some level of aggression.

In Britain at this time the rituals concerned with the disposal of the dead have left little or no archaeological trace and we are therefore robbed of burial evidence comparable to that of the Continent, but the very existence of swords and horse gear of Continental type is sufficient to suggest the presence of mounted warriors. This type of equipment has been found across most regions of Britain. While this implies the widespread recognition of warrior gear as a measure of status it does not necessarily mean that warfare was equally distributed.

It was during the seventh and sixth centuries that hillforts sprang up in considerable numbers. They were particularly dense in central southern Britain but spread outside this zone both to east and west. There can be little

71 *Slingers defending the ramparts of an Iron Age fort. The sling was a cheap but highly effective weapon. Huge quantities of sling stones have been found on some hillforts, e.g., Maiden Castle and Danebury.*

doubt that, unlike their predecessors the hilltop enclosures, the early hillforts were designed to withstand attack and there is evidence to suggest that some were actually attacked and may have been destroyed. At Danebury, both gates of the early hillfort showed signs of having been burnt. This, in itself, is not sufficient to imply destruction by hostile forces since it could equally convincingly be argued that the burning of gates may have been a symbolic act carried out by the occupants. However, in broadly contemporary layers immediately behind the rampart on the south side of the enclosure very large numbers of carefully selected pebbles, roughly 3cm (1–1¼in.) across, were found. These are likely to have served as sling stones and were brought to the site from a source several kilometres away. The sling was a very efficient weapon (**71**). It was cheap to make, needing only a few thongs of leather and could be used with deadly accuracy – as Goliath was momentarily to realize. Wielded by defenders manning the top of a rampart and protected by a breastwork of some kind, it was the ideal weapon to drive off attackers who would

be entirely exposed in their approach. Fired in an overarm trajectory vollies of sling stones could be made to rain down like artillery fire gaining momentum from the fall. Shot from a horizontal motion they could accurately pick off an attacker up to a range of about 60m (*c.* 130ft).

The combination of the bank and ditch defence and the sling would have ensured the comparative security of hillforts in time of attack. While it is quite reasonable to argue (as we have above, pp. 50) that hillforts were designed to be symbols of power and dominance, it would be quite wrong to underestimate their purely defensive role.

If then the flowering of hillfort building in the seventh and sixth centuries and the appearance of the accoutrements of the mounted warrior at the same time are related to a period of widespread social unrest accompanied by raiding, the demise of the hillfort in most of the country except the central southern region could mean that the zone of unrest became more restricted after the fifth century. However, once fort building had begun in the centre south, certain forts were maintained and developed increasingly strong defences. While this must, in part, reflect the continued use of the fort as a symbol of communal unity and strength, it must surely mean that the forts retained a defensive role. The size, and in some cases the number, of the ramparts and ditches would have given added strength; so too would the elaboration of the entrances.

Entrances were the weak spots where any attack is likely to have focused. Several cases are known in the central southern zone where second entrances were blocked leaving only one (e.g. Danebury (Hants.), Beacon Hill (Hants.), Uffington Castle (Berks)). This may have been one response to the problem; another was to strengthen the entrance with hornworks flanking the way to the gate, to create a long funnel-like approach so that anyone who wished to enter the fort would have to pass along a corridor constricted by high ramparts

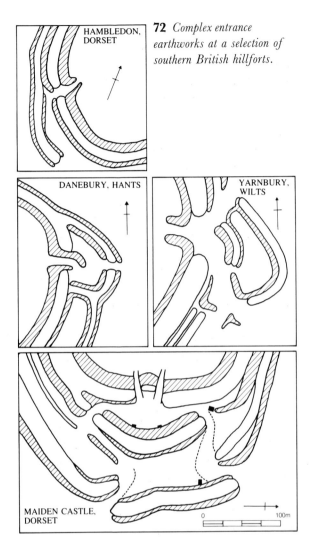

72 *Complex entrance earthworks at a selection of southern British hillforts.*

inner hornwork was constructed partly to create the narrow corridor leading to the gate itself and partly to form a flat-topped platform in the centre of the entrance complex, from which defenders with slings could oversee the approaches and the flanks of the main earthworks, as well as commanding an outer gate immediately in front of them set between two claw-like outer earthworks. The entire complex must have been designed primarily from a defensive point of view although to any visitor it would also have been dauntingly impressive. That defence was a reality is clearly shown by the thousands of sling stones found on and around the inner hornwork and the dump of 6000 or so in a pit just inside the gate. Some time around 100 BC or just after, the gate was completely consumed by fire: even the buried stumps of the gate timbers, 60cm (2ft) in diameter, were thoroughly burned through. Such a massive fire is hardly likely to have been accidental but between the two possible explanations – deliberate demolition by the inhabitants in some kind of symbolic end or destruction by an enemy – it is impossible to choose. It is, however, relevant to recall here Julius Caesar's description of native attacks on hillforts:

> The Gauls and the Belgae use the same method of attack. They surround the whole circuit of the walls with a large number of men and shower it with stones from all sides, so that the defences are denuded of men. Then they form *testudo*, set fire to the gates and undermine the walls.

In summary, the developed hillforts of the centre south very probably reflect an unstable situation in which waves of aggression are likely to have swept over the countryside from time to time. When raids were imminent the forts would have been put into defensive readiness; on other occasions life would have continued at a more relaxed pace (**colour plate 3**).

Something of the reality of these phases of aggression is provided by the study of the

(**72**). One method, widely adopted to achieve this, was to turn the ends of the rampart inwards to form a corridor and to place the gate at the end. Other techniques to increase the length of the approach involved overlapping the ditch ends in an *en échelon* fashion (e.g. at Hod Hill in Dorset) or constructing pincer-like foreworks as at Danebury. The most complex works of this kind to be built were the colossal entrance approaches of Maiden Castle. But in all cases we must stress that, alongside defensive considerations, there must always have been the desire to impress.

The Danebury gate provides an example of a comparatively modest entrance. Here an

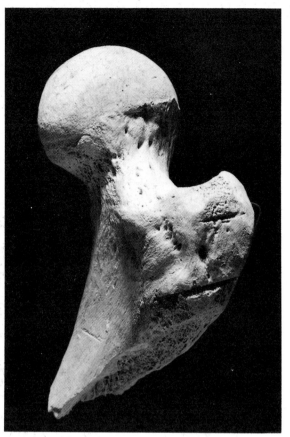

73 *The head of a human femur from Danebury showing a variety of cuts resulting from sword slashes to the hip.*

rather meagre sample of human bones recovered from excavations: violent death and mutilation are widely in evidence. From Danebury at least ten individuals were identified who had suffered injuries from swords or other weapons and of these only two had survived (**73, 74**). Invariably the wounds were found on young males and most usually it was the skull that had suffered – five with sword slashes, three with spears or other sharp points and one with a blunt weapon. When it is remembered how easy it is to kill by stabbing the soft parts of the abdomen leaving no trace on the bones, then the likelihood is that the incidence of violent death was high.

The archaeological record of the Middle and Late Iron Age provides ample evidence of the accoutrements of war – swords, shields, spears,

helmets and vehicle parts. The majority are from hoards or votive deposits but a small group of burials provides valuable evidence about the way in which the warrior was equipped (**64**). The normal method, similar to that found widely on the Continent, is exemplified by the inhumation from Owslebury, Hants. Here the warrior is laid on his back with his sword close to his right side and the spear to the left. The shield, of which only the central bronze boss survived, had been placed over the body. The wearing of the sword on the right-hand side of the body is known from Continental burials and from iconographic evidence. An exactly similar arrangement was found in a grave at Kings Road, Guernsey. Other British warrior burials show variations on this arrangement. At Grimthorpe in Yorkshire the body was crouched lying on its left side with the sword and spear in front and the shield above, while at Whitcombe in Dorset the body was crouched but on its right side with weapons to the front. No evidence of the shield survived but it could have been made entirely of wood and leather, in which case there would have been no tangible remains.

In south Yorkshire a number of burials of the Arras Culture have been found with weapons but not with a complete working set. In the cemetery at Rudston three burials had only a sword, two a dagger, five a spearhead and one a shield, while at Kirkburn one of the warriors was provided with only a tunic of mail. In most of these burials accompanied by a sword, the sword was found beneath the body or at its back in the case of those buried on their side. That the sword was actually worn on the back is shown by a collection of stone figurines found in the area (**75**). The depiction is particularly clear in the case of the carvings from Wetwang Slack, Withernsea and Malton. Differences in the way in which armour was worn are more likely to be statements of ethnicity than to reflect different modes of fighting.

The Arras Culture burials provide the best evidence available in Britain for two-wheeled

74 *Mutilated and dismembered bodies thrown into a pit at Danebury.*

vehicles: 14 are known, of which six have now been excavated under modern archaeological conditions. In each case there is clear evidence that the vehicle, used presumably to take the dead person to the grave, had been carefully dismantled. First the wheels were removed and placed flat on the floor of the grave pit with the body laid out above. Then the T-shaped framework – the axle and pole – was placed on top, with the box-shaped body of the vehicle set above upside down to form a cover. The yoke was placed next to the body to the west.

Although it is tempting to regard these vehicles as chariots, and the burials as those of aristocratic charioteers, the weight of evidence is against this. Only three of the 14 or so adequately recorded vehicle burials were accompanied by weapons and, as we have noted previously (p. 80), the rite was not restricted to males. More to the point, the box-shaped body of the vehicle would probably have been far too heavy for a war chariot, which is more likely to have had a much simpler platform comprising a light wooden frame and hide base. It is simpler therefore to regard the Yorkshire vehicles as carts, perhaps specifically related to the stately transport of the elite – alive or dead. These vehicles, and for that matter the few burials with warrior equipment, cannot therefore be taken to indicate warlike conditions among the Arras Culture. Indeed in

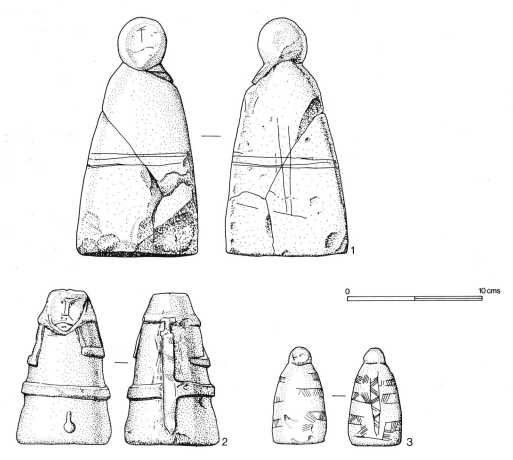

75 *Stone figurines from North Humberside, each showing the sword being worn in the centre of the back, in a manner reflected in some contemporary burials.*

a recent detailed analysis of 246 skeletons from four Yorkshire cemeteries (Rudston, Burton Fleming, Garton Station and Kirkburn) no evidence of sword slashes were noted on any of the bones, in marked contrast to the sample from Danebury. The only *possible* examples of violent death were three bodies found with spears in them but this situation could have resulted from the rite of spearing bodies at the time of burial – a practice noted in other graves in the region.

If then the Yorkshire vehicles were not war chariots, it raises the question of what the vehicles referred to by Caesar were really like. Schematic visual representations of war chariots are known on several coins of the first century BC, the clearest on a gold stater of the northern Gaulish tribe, the Remi, minted in *c.* 60 BC, and on a Roman denarius of Hostilius Sasserna minted about ten years later. Both show a light-bodied structure open at the front and back but with the sides guarded by a double inverted U-framework of bent wood. An exactly similar arrangement is shown on two grave stelae from Padua dating to the third century BC. The only real difference between the Arras vehicles and these war chariots lies in the nature of the body structure: the basic construction is the same for both and it therefore remains a distinct possibility that the chassis could have been adapted for either purpose. The possibility of the dual function would have been clearly understood by those observing the funerary rituals in southern Yorkshire. Thus to be carried to the grave in such a vehicle would have been to endow the deceased with an

1 *(Left) Small islands in lakes, either natural or artificially created, were often used for settlements, as in this case at Esha Ness on Shetland* (copyright: the author).

2 *(Below) The Iron Age settlement at Gurness, on Orkney, clusters around a broch. Good timber for building is rare on the island so the inhabitants had to use stone for all the internal fittings as well as for the structures* (copyright: the author).

3 *(Above) The hillfort of Flowers Barrow occupies a dramatic site on the coast of Dorset, dominating the Isle of Purbeck. The banks and ditches which defend the settlement were restructured on a number of occasions, suggesting a long period of use* (copyright: the author).

4 *(Left) The hillfort of Uffington sits high on the Berkshire Downs, looking down on the vale of Oxfordshire. In its original state, probably in the fifth century BC, it had two entrances but one was subsequently blocked* (copyright: the Institute of Archaeology, Oxford).

5 *(Right) The small bronze attachment from Stanwick in Yorkshire is a masterpiece of 'Celtic' art. By using two simple trumpet scrolls the craftsman has managed to create a brilliant evocation of a doleful horse* (copyright: British Museum).

8 (*Left*) *The hillfort of Danebury, Hampshire, from the air. The defences of the hillfort, occupied from the sixth to the first centuries* BC, *lie within a larger enclosure which was probably constructed in the Late Bronze Age, possibly as a place where livestock was collected together at certain times during the year* (copyright: Danebury Trust).

6 *(Above) The village of Chysauster in Cornwall is still extremely well preserved. Occupation probably began in the Iron Age and continued well into the Roman period. The individual houses with their garden plots, cluster along a street (drawn by Judith Dobie; copyright: English Heritage).*

7 *A 'Celtic' feast in full flight (drawn by Chris Evans; copyright: English Heritage).*

9 *Danebury was destroyed by fire during the first century BC. Some of the latest pits have produced multiple burials. Whether they represent people killed in an attack or a ritual deposit of some kind is unclear (copyright: Danebury Trust).*

10 (Left) Hengistbury Head in Dorset became an important port in the first century BC. The archaeological evidence shows that large numbers of Italian wine amphorae were imported, no doubt in exchange for raw materials and slaves (drawn by Chris Evans; copyright: English Heritage).

11 (Above) Broken fragments of a gold torc found at Hengistbury. Metals of all kinds were brought together here, probably for export in the first century BC (copyright: Institute of Archaeology, Oxford).

12 (Right) Reconstruction of an Iron Age warrior of the first century BC from the Museum of the Iron Age at Andover. All the details are based on archaeological or documentary evidence (copyright: Hampshire County Museum Services).

13 *The chariot was an important feature of Celtic warfare. Julius Caesar
gives a vivid description of the Britons' highly effective use of chariots when
he campaigned in Britain in 55 and 54 BC* (drawn by Chris Evans;
copyright: English Heritage).

authority embedded in the idea, if not the actuality, of military prestige.

Taking, then, a broad view of the Middle Iron Age in Britain, there are cogent reasons to argue that in the centre south endemic warfare, resulting in sporadic raids, was an ever-present reality, whereas in the rest of Britain a generally more stable situation could well have persisted. Even so the symbols of military prowess are likely to have been maintained and rivalries leading sometimes to outright aggression are almost certain to have flared up from time to time.

If this picture of Britain in the period 400–100 BC approximates to the truth, then Britain must have been far more stable than much of the adjacent Continent, where hordes of warriors rampaged far and wide and whole communities uprooted themselves to engage in ambitious migrations.

There does, however, seem to be something of a mismatch between this picture of Middle Iron Age Britain, with its single zone of warring marcher lords creating a corridor of instability through central southern Britain, and the turmoil which preceded the Caesarian invasion and made the large-scale mobilization of large armies possible. These differences may be the result of our inadequate perceptions but it is worth exploring other possibilities before taking the easy way out.

The slave trade

The one factor of overriding importance which imposed itself upon the British Isles in the period c. 120–60 BC was the actuality, albeit distant and unquantified, of the Roman consumer market. Huge volumes of raw materials and large numbers of slaves were required in increasing quantities to fuel the Roman economy throughout this period and, indeed,

it is possible to interpret the exploits of Caesar and Pompey as motivated, indirectly perhaps, by the need to satisfy these demands. Time and time again Strabo refers to the consumption of slaves, and slaves are one of the commodities which he specifically lists as among the exports of Britain. There is no way in which, archaeologically, we will be able to demonstrate the volume of this export. One slave chain has been found in a bog on Anglesey (**62**) and another at the hillfort of Bigbury in Kent but two slave chains hardly make an export industry. However, we have only to look at the situation in west Africa in the seventeenth and eighteenth centuries to see what a devastating social and economic effect on indigenous societies the American consumer market in slaves could have.

If the export of slaves from Britain in the period c. 120–60 BC was on any scale it is bound to have had an effect on south-eastern societies. Before the contact period there was no market in slaves, though servile labour may well have featured in local social systems. If, then, a slave suddenly became a marketable commodity, and one that could be exchanged for luxury goods, then there was a real impetus to their acquisition. The traditional way in which this was achieved was by raiding. In other words it is *possible* that the proximity of the Roman market encouraged native communities to generate slaves as a new cash crop. In a society where endemic warfare was part of the social system, even though it may have been transmuted into a more symbolic phase, the new opportunities may have unleashed old enthusiasms. Some such model could explain the social turmoil and warlike preparedness which Caesar encountered. The least that can be said of these speculations is that they lie within the realms of possibility.

8

Approaching the gods

The world of the Iron Age was pervaded by the gods. Everywhere there would have been visual reminders of their power, and no activity, however trivial, would have been entered into without some thought for the attitudes of those who inhabited the other world. In this the Iron Age communities were probably no different from most primitive or underdeveloped societies. To untangle the mass of detail available from excavations, iconography, classical texts and, more rarely, from place names, and build it into some semblance of a system is not easy. We must remember that generalized schemes constructed in this way may not always have had equal relevance in all regions but, this said, a remarkably coherent picture can be created if the Gaulish evidence is used alongside the British.

The year's calendar

One vitally important concept was that of time. Animals, human or otherwise, are conscious of the passage of time and it is in the nature of human beings that they should wish to 'control' time by containing it within a system of measurement. This becomes even more practically important as the growing of crops begins to play an increasingly central part in the subsistence economy. By the Iron Age the passage of time – the year with its seasons demarcated – was rigorously controlled with a calendar.

Remarkable evidence of this was found at Coligny near Bourg, in France, in the form of

fragments of an actual bronze calendar dating to the end of the first century BC. It was divided into sixteen columns representing 62 lunar months and two intercalary months. Each of the months was divided into 28 or 29 days arranged in two sets, the dark half and the bright half, separated by the word *atenoux* meaning the returning light. There is also an indication of whether the month is propitious (*mat*) or unpropitious (*anm*) – information essential for anyone planning to embark upon an enterprise. The calendar is also inscribed with the position of two of the four great seasonal festivals – Beltane (1 May) and Lugnasad (1 August). Beltane marked the beginning of the warm season when cattle would be turned out to open grazing, while Lugnasad, named after the god Lug, seems to have been connected with rituals to ensure the ripening of the crops. The two other festivals of the Celtic year were Samain (1 November) and Imbolc (1 February), both known from Irish vernacular sources of the first millennium AD but nonetheless likely to have been practised in the earlier prehistoric period. Samain marks the end of the one year and the beginning of the next – it was an inbetween time, a liminal period, and therefore dangerous. All this is reflected in more recent beliefs embedded in Hallowe'en and the Christianized version of All Souls when, briefly, the spirits of the dead are set loose. In the agrarian cycle it represents the time when the grazing season was over and the flocks and herds were brought in for culling. Less is known of Imbolc but it may have been the time of year when the ewes began lactation, indicating the first beginnings of the new regenerative cycle.

This four-fold division of the year was very probably of great antiquity, going back perhaps as far as the Neolithic period. It is still echoed today in European folk culture. Imbolc and Samain have been Christianized as the feasts of St Brigit and All Souls, while both Beltane and Samain retain their pagan flavour as May Day and Hallowe'en. Only Lugnasad has lost its significance.

It is easy to appreciate how, for a people whose very being was rooted in the agrarian cycle, the festivals marking the progress of the year were vital indicators of the passing of time. They were the occasions when the various gods were acknowledged and placated. The dark half of the year began on 1 November with the feast of Samain when, in Irish tradition, the tribal god Dagda mated with the earth mother goddess Morrígan, their successful union ensuring universal fertility and general well-being in the year to come. The dark half ended and the light half began on 1 May at the feast of Beltane with its symbolism of fire and purification and a sense of forward-looking to the feasting and relaxation which followed the end of the arduous period of caring for the crops, culminating in the harvest when new supplies of food were brought in safely from the fields. This simple cycle, no doubt embroidered around with a complex pattern of beliefs and rituals, varying from region to region and time to time, will have provided a reassuring structure within which to arrange both the practical and religious aspects of a life.

How important were lunar and solar cycles during the Iron Age is very difficult to say. In all probability the midsummer and midwinter solstices were acknowledged but there is little evidence for this either in the archaeological record or the classical or vernacular literature. Indeed, it may well be that the massive change of emphasis towards controlling the land and its productive capacity, which we have identified as beginning in the late second millennium in Britain, saw a major shift from a religious system based on astronomical phenomena to one focused on the agrarian cycle.

Celtic deities

There is abundant evidence of a confusingly large number of deities worshipped in western Europe. In his generalizations about Gaulish religion Caesar says that:

> The god they worship most is Mercury, and they have very many images of him. They regard him as the inventor of all the arts, the guide of all their roads and journeys and the god who has greatest power for trading and money making.

He then goes on to say that they worship other gods – Apollo, Mars, Jupiter and Minerva. We need not take this too literally. Caesar was simply observing a great variety of native deities and attempting to relate them by attribute to the deities of the classical pantheon which would have been familiar to his readers but his singling out of one, 'Mercury', 'inventor of all arts', is an interesting reflection of the Irish deity Dagda whose name means 'the all-competent'. Perhaps here and in particular in the Irish pairing of Dagda and Morrígan we are able to glimpse the underlying structure of the Iron Age belief system – a simple pairing of opposites: male/sky/tribal/all-competent with female/earth/universal/all-fertile. If this is so, then the great variety of male deities simply reflects the different tribal gods, while the many female deities are manifestations of the one earth mother seen in various local guises. The generalization is probably close to the truth but divergent traditions, developing over long periods of time, will have led to the same confusing variety that we see today among the different Christian demi-gods or saints with their regional concentrations and their widely varying attributes.

The Roman poet Lucan, writing in the first century AD, mentions the names of three Gaulish gods, Taranis, Teutates and Eusus. In Celtic Taranis means 'thunder', Teutates means 'the people', while Eusus is very probably cognate with 'master'. In these three names alone are the attributes of the generalized male god – sky/tribe/all-competent. The female deity – the earth mother – is frequently associated with springs, for example Sulis at Bath and Sequanna at the source of the Seine in Burgundy. The spring is the place where the underworld communicates with our world and it is quite logical therefore that it is considered to be the location where it is easiest to make contact with the deity. The long continuity of this tradition is reflected in French river names, the majority of which are female, and in the very large numbers of springs and wells in the west of Britain and in Ireland which are today presided over by Christian female saints.

Sacrifice and offerings

Caesar was quite specific over the need to placate the deities with sacrifices and offerings:

> The Gauls believe the power of the gods can only be appeased if one human life is exchanged for another and they have sacrifices of this kind regularly established by the community.... They believe that the gods prefer it if the people executed have been caught in the act of theft or armed robbery or some other crime, but when the supply of victims runs out, they even go to the extent of sacrificing innocent men.

He mentions, too, the extremely superstitious nature of the Gauls who, if seriously ill or facing danger, promise to make a human sacrifice. Similarly, after a successful battle they dedicate the spoils to the gods.

> They sacrifice the captured animals and collect all the rest of the spoils in one place. Among many of the tribes it is possible to see piles of these objects on consecrated ground.

Anyone who dared to hide booty at home or steal from the trophy heap would be put to death by the most terrible torture.

In southern Gaul, in the vicinity of Toulouse, so Posidonius records, immense amounts of treasure estimated to include 100,000lb (*c.* 45,000kg) of gold and 110,000lb (*c.* 50,000kg) of silver were stacked up in the sacred precincts and deposited in pools, totally safe from predators – until, that is, the Roman Consul Caepio pillaged the lot in 106 BC.

The archaeological evidence from Britain provides interesting potential confirmation of these practices, though it is not, of course, possible to ascribe motives to the acts of depositions which have been recorded. One of the most dramatic discoveries of recent years has been the recovery of much of a well-preserved body found in a peat bog at Lindow in Cheshire (**8**). The individual, a young male, had been struck violently on the head, was strangled and had had his throat cut: in other words he had been 'killed' in three separate ways. Here surely is evidence of ritual murder and the deposition of the corpse in a bog suggests a dedication to the deities of the underworld.

More difficult to interpret are the skeletons found on the bottoms of disused storage pits, of which the hillfort of Danebury has provided a large sample (below, p. 103). They lie in a variety of positions (**76, colour plate 9**) but quite often with wrists together, suggesting that they may have been tied. In some cases the bodies have had large flints and blocks of chalk laid or thrown on to them. These too could have been the victims of ritual killings, their bodies placed as offerings to the earth deities, though of course other explanations are possible. No evidence survives of the manner of death but strangling, throat-cutting or even stoning or burial alive are all possibilities.

In the cases of bodies placed in bogs or in pits, it is tempting to see them as propitiatory offerings made to the deities of the earth and therefore possibly associated in some way with fertility. If so, it is reasonable to ask if there is

76 *Human body in the bottom of a disused storage pit in Danebury. Such deposits are probably propitiatory burials.*

any evidence of offerings to the male, tribal, deities of the sky. Here Caesar's reference to sacrifice by burning may be relevant. Some communities, he says, have huge cages of wickerwork which are filled with living men and then set on fire. Such a practice is likely to be difficult to detect archaeologically.

The deposition of the spoils of war as heaped-up trophies on land stand little chance of surviving, but there are numerous instances of metalwork of military character recovered from watery contexts. Most relevant to the discussion is the amazing collection of metal items recovered from a bog at Llyn Cerrig Bach on Anglesey. The pieces seem to have been thrown from a rock platform into what was then a lake. Besides spears, swords and shields the find included a range of horse trappings and vehicle fittings, tools, a slave chain, part of a trumpet and a number of other smaller items. Here, presumably, we are looking on a collection of gear, quite possibly assembled as the result of a battle, which was deliberately thrown into the water to placate the deities.

Less certainty attaches to the large numbers of weapons found in rivers, particularly the Thames, including famous pieces like the Battersea and Wandsworth shields, the horned helmet from Waterloo Bridge and the many fine swords and daggers. A high percentage of these pieces are of the very highest quality and must have been aristocratic equipment of extreme value. While it remains an uncomfortable possibility that only the best and most obviously ancient pieces were retained by those who observed the dredgings in the eighteenth and nineteenth centuries, and thus a full spectrum of material had originally been thrown into the river, a more plausible explanation is that here we are seeing the more selective deposition of objects of high value made during individual acts of dedication.

Different again are the remarkable hoards of gold torcs found in East Anglia of which Snettisham presents the greatest variety. Here, in a limited area no less than 11 separate depositions in small, specially dug pits have been recovered, each consisting of several items, most usually gold or electrum torcs entire or broken. Under what circumstances these deposits came to be made is a matter of debate but the most likely possibility is that they were votive deposits buried within a circumscribed sacred zone. The restriction of deposits of this kind to East Anglia hints at a distinct regionalization in ritual practice.

The river deposits may also show some degree of regionalism in that the great majority of river finds come from east-flowing rivers, in particular the Thames, Witham, Trent and Tyne. The south-flowing and west-flowing rivers have produced virtually no votive items. While this may, in part, be the result of an accident of survival (e.g. the east-flowing rivers may have seen more nineteenth-century dredging than the west), the pattern is sufficiently marked to suggest that some rivers were more prone to receive offerings than others and of these the Thames was outstanding. It may not, therefore, be too fanciful to suggest that some rivers may, in the Iron Age, have been regarded as particularly sacred. It is even possible that the male connotations associated with the Thames in more recent folklore ('Old Father Thames') might be an echo of the male/warrior/tribal attributes of the Iron Age, reflected in the masses of weaponry thrown into it.

The counterpart of the river deposits of the east are the bog and lake deposits of the west, of which Llyn Cerrig Bach is an example already mentioned. Here again it may be that the comparatively large number of these

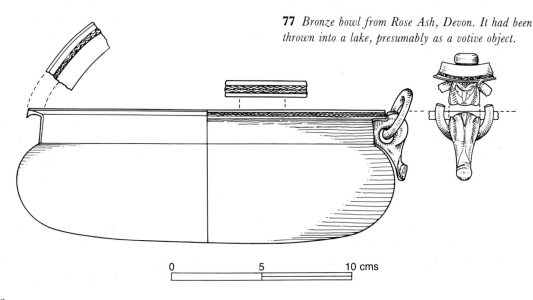

77 *Bronze bowl from Rose Ash, Devon. It had been thrown into a lake, presumably as a votive object.*

0   5   10 cms

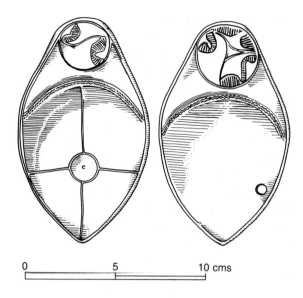

0   5   10 cms

78 *A pair of bronze spoons found in a bog at Crosby Ravensworth, Westmorland. Pairs of spoons of this kind were probably ritual objects.*

dogs were usually buried entire, horses were partially dismembered, horse heads and horse legs being particularly common but occasionally a carcass less the head or a leg or two was deposited. These special deposits are not restricted to farmyard animals. Human bodies were sometimes found, as were collections of pottery or other items such as horse gear.

Special deposits of this kind were usually found on the bottoms of pits and must therefore have been placed very soon after the grain stored in the pit had been removed. Thereafter the majority of the pits were left open for a while, allowing the sides to begin to erode, and after this period there is often evidence of a second deposit of domestic material, such as animal remains, quernstones, stone or clay weights, etc., having been made before the pit was abandoned altogether or deliberately filled. While this pattern is by no means universal it is found sufficiently frequently to suggest that it reflects a distinct and restricted set of behaviour.

It is one thing to observe patterns of this kind and quite another to explain them, given the absence of any documentary evidence. Nevertheless it is possible to interpret the evidence in terms of fertility and propitiation. The pits were probably dug specifically to store seed grain between harvest and sowing. This would have required them to be sealed with chalk marl or daub to prevent air from getting in and would incidentally have made pit storage quite unsuitable for consumption grain – to which access was required on a regular basis. The digging of the pit and the placing of the seed corn in it was very probably an act endowed with deep religious meaning – the seed corn was, appropriately, being placed in the realms of the chthonic deities controlling fertility and the underworld. It would have been necessary, then, once the seed had been removed and sown, to have made a propitiatory offering to the deity in thanks for safely keeping the seed through the dangerous liminal period of quiescence and in anticipation of successful germination. Thus the primary offering would

deposits in the west is merely a reflection of the prevalence of bogs and lakes in the region but another element in the patterning is the more frequent occurrence of containers in these contexts, items such as cauldrons, bowls and tankards (**77, 78**). The evidence is tenuous but here again we may be observing a regional pattern.

The gold deposits of East Anglia are not the only example of earth-bound depositions: indeed recent work has shown that deliberately placed deposits occur widely on settlement sites, usually in disused grain storage pits. The phenomenon is sufficiently curious to deserve some consideration. The excavation of a large sample of storage pits within the hillfort of Danebury has enabled distinct patterns of deposition to be recognized, the most obvious being the placing of animal carcasses, in whole or in part, usually on the bottoms of the pits. Although all the usual domesticated animals are treated in this way a distinct preference was shown to horses and dogs (**79**) – and, among birds, to ravens. All three played a special part in Celtic religion and their selection for deposition can hardly be accidental. While

79 *A propitiatory burial from a pit at Danebury. The complete body of a dog was placed around a severed horse leg.*

probably have been made in the spring, the pit thereafter being left open to silt up.

Possibly, of course, these deposits were all made together at the time of the appropriate ceremony, in this case presumably Beltane (1 May), which could explain why in some of the pits silt had begun to form before the special deposit was made. This raises the possibility that the second deposit may also have been made at the time of one of the seasonal festivals – perhaps Lugnasad (1 August) in anticipation of, or in response to, a successful harvest, or Samain (1 November) when harvests, flocks and herds had been safely gathered in.

Although this explanation is essentially speculative there is, in Indo-European tradition, a well-formed belief in the importance of the pit as a means of reaching the chthonic deities and where propitiatory offerings were to be made. To the Greeks this was the *bothros* and to the Romans the *mundus*. A special kind of sacred pit, where items used in sacrifices including the bones and ashes of the sacrifices themselves were put, was called the *favissa*. Moreover in the Greek legend of Proserpine, who has to spend part of the year underground before emerging to sow the corn, classical scholars have argued that we are seeing a myth embodying the concept of the seed corn being stored underground in the protection of the deity of the underworld. There is nothing unreasonable in supposing that broad belief systems of this kind pervaded Europe, to appear with distinctive local characteristics from place to place and time to time.

If we are correct in supposing that pit storage reflects a particular belief system, it is interesting to note that it began to become widespread only in the Early Iron Age. Thus it may be another aspect of the greater emphasis being placed at this time on the productive capacity of the soil. A final point worth making is that pit storage was of restricted distribution, concentrating on the central southern zone of Britain. It is tempting to see this as a reflection of the extent of the area over which this particular belief system held sway.

The Druids

In most societies intermediaries exist between men and the gods. In Iron Age Europe this position was occupied by the Druids who were held in high esteem, according to Caesar equal to the Knights. Caesar is quite explicit about their function:

> They have control over public and private sacrifices and give rulings on all religious questions. Large numbers of young men go to them for instruction ... and they are greatly honoured by the people. In almost all disputes, between communities or between individuals the Druids act as judges.... Any individual or community not abiding by their verdict is banned from the sacrifices, and this is regarded among the Gauls as the most severe punishment. Those who are banned in this way are reckoned as sacrilegious criminals. Everyone shuns them; no one will go near or speak to them for fear of becoming contaminated in some way by contact with them.

In this passage the essence of the power of the religious elite is neatly summed up. No one can approach the gods without their intercession and their disapproval leads to ostracization. Caesar goes on to describe the rigorous nature of the training, which requires initiates to study for 20 years, committing all their learning to memory.

It would seem that by Caesar's time the Druids of Gaul belonged to a single extra-tribal brotherhood sufficiently organized to hold an annual meeting at a sacred location in the territory of the Carnutes and to be governed by a single elected leader. This unified organization, combined with their coercive powers, would have posed a considerable threat to the Roman conquest and it was probably for this reason that the Romans were unusually vehement in their condemnation of the religious order.

To what extent the Druidic organization in Gaul can be thought to mirror that of Britain is unclear but Caesar makes a most intriguing observation almost as an aside:

> It is thought that the doctrine of the Druids was invested in Britain and was brought from there into Gaul: even today those who want to study the doctrine in greater detail usually go to Britain to learn there.

While this may all be true, in which case it could be argued that the tradition goes back to the great phase of monumental religious building beginning in the mid-third millennium and culminating with the trilithons of Stonehenge, a more sober interpretation would be that the isolated nature of the British Isles allowed the belief system to develop in a distinctive and intensified form, thought by contemporary Gauls to represent a purer or more orthodox strain. At any event we may take it that Druidic beliefs were alive and well in Britain.

Druids were certainly in evidence in AD 60 when the Roman commander Suetonius Paulinus decided to flush out dissidents who had fled to the Isle of Anglesey (*Mona*). The occasion is vividly described by Tacitus:

> The shore was lined by a motley battle array. There were warriors with their arms, and women rushing to and fro among their ranks,

dressed in black, like Furies, their hair dishevelled, brandishing torches, and Druids with their arms raised to heaven calling down terrible curses.

Roman might prevailed and the defenders were cut to pieces. One of the first tasks of the garrison placed to control the island was to destroy the religious centres.

The groves sacred to savage rites were cut down, for their religion enjoined them to drench their altars with the blood of prisoners and to find out the will of the gods by consulting the entrails of human beings.

Always allowing the Roman desire to over-exaggerate the barbarian nature of their opponents to justify their conquests, this reference to divination using human victims is echoed in earlier Greek ethnographies describing Gauls in the second and first centuries BC,

80 *Wooden figurine, possibly Epona the horse goddess, well known in Gaul. Found at Lower Brook Street, Winchester in an early second century AD context.*

and it is not unlikely that rituals of this kind remained in operation in outlying parts of the British Isles: times of tension often exacerbate superstitious behaviour.

Of the Druids themselves in Britain there is no archaeological evidence. Two burials found in a cemetery at Deal in Kent, one with a pair of spoons of ritual character, the other wearing a diadem, are sufficiently unusual to suggest that they may have been of religious personages but the evidence is inconclusive.

The classical texts give the general impression that religious sites were open-air locations, often clearings in woods and without structures other than altars or old tree trunks carved in the form of idols (**80**). There is, however, an increasing body of archaeological evidence to suggest that built shrines were not at all uncommon. Two types are now known, rectangular and circular. The most convincing of the rectangular sanctuaries was found at Heathrow, Middlesex. Here a small *cella* was sited within a surround of post-holes, which (if contemporary) may well have created an ambulatory. The plan has close similarities to the plans of Romano-Celtic temples found scattered over most of western Europe after the Roman conquest and it could well be that the Heathrow type of shrine was equally widespread in the pre-Roman period. Other rather simpler examples comprising just the rectangular *cella* have been found in the hillforts of South Cadbury and Danebury and also on Lancing Down in Sussex close to a later Roman temple, here suggesting a continuity of religious function. An even more remarkable example of continuity was found on Hayling Island (**81**) where a circular timber shrine, set within a rectangular fenced *temenos* (enclosure) and dating to the Late Iron Age, was rebuilt to almost exactly the same plan in masonry in the late first century AD, several decades after the invasion. Another example of what may have been a circular sanctuary being rebuilt in masonry is known in the centre of Maiden Castle.

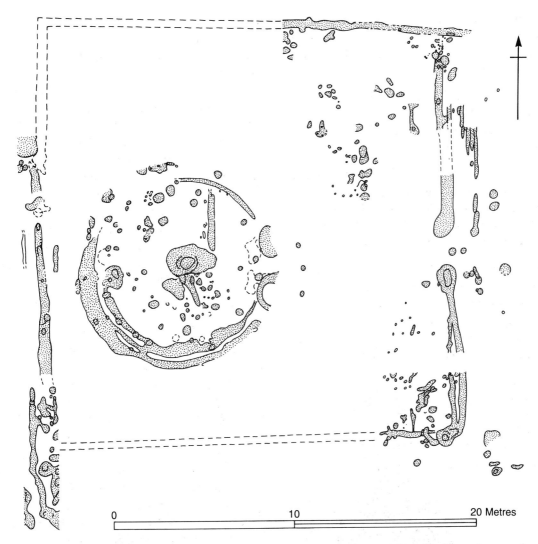

81 *A circular temple of the Late Iron Age set within a rectangular precinct, found at Hayling Island, Hampshire. The exact plan was replicated in stone when the temple was rebuilt in the late first century* AD.

From scattered evidence of this kind it is clear that not only were there many fixed religious locations in Britain focusing around small timber-built shrines but that many, if not most, of these sites continued to be revered into and throughout the Roman period.

One of the most enduring of the sacred locations known in Britain is the hot spring at Bath. Here, on a low spur surrounded on three sides by the River Avon, a persistent spring of hot mineral water breaks through, pouring out a quarter of a million gallons of water a day at a temperature of 45°C. Little is known of the arrangement of the spring in the pre-Roman period but excavations have exposed a causeway of gravel and boulders built out through the surrounding mud to the focus of the spring, and in the sediments around were found a number of Celtic coins most of them of the local tribe the Dobunni (**82**). The spring was sacred to a female deity, Sulis, later under Roman guidance conflated with Minerva, no doubt in recognition that both shared the same attributes of healing and wisdom. The evident power and importance of the native sanctuary is amply

82 *Excavation in progress in the Roman spring in Bath. The gravel in the bottom right is a causeway constructed to the spring head in the Late Iron Age. The spring was sacred to the goddess Sulis.*

demonstrated by the elaborate way in which the Romans treated it, turning it into one of the foremost healing sanctuaries of western Europe. The sanctuary at Bath known to the Romans as *Aquae Sulis* provides us with a rare example of the name and powers of a native goddess.

Death

Of the attitudes of the Gauls to death Caesar was quite explicit:

> The Druids attach particular importance to the belief that the soul does not perish but passes after death from one body to another: they think that this belief is the most effective way to encourage bravery because it removes the fear of death...although Gaul is not a rich country, funerals there are splendid and costly. Everything the dead man is thought to have been fond of is put on the pyre,

including even animals. Not long ago slaves and dependants known to have been their masters' favourites were burned with them at the end of the funeral.

Belief in the afterlife reflected in the burial of grave goods, was as we have seen, a feature of the south-east of Britain in the last century or so before the Roman invasion. It was here, too, that the rite of cremation, prevalent at the time on the Continent, was widely favoured at all levels in society. But the comparatively restricted distribution in Britain of the archaeological manifestations of the very generalized Gaulish system, as described by Caesar, is a firm reminder that attitudes to death can vary considerably from one location to another and with time.

Only in southern Yorkshire, in the territory of the so-called Arras Culture, does the archaeological record suggest a 'normal' system of disposal of the dead in large, sometimes very large, inhumation cemeteries. Here, the range of status implied by the grave goods and the age and gender profiles of the deceased, all suggest that the Arras cemeteries reflect the entire population. Moreover, the burials are so numerous as to suggest that cemetery inhumation was the only significant means of disposal.

In the south-west peninsula a few organized inhumation cemeteries have also been found (**83**), the largest being at Harlyn Bay on the north coast of Cornwall where many stone-lined graves have been uncovered. Graves of this kind have been found elsewhere in the south-west but the total number is very small.

In the rest of the British Isles burial by inhumation or cremation is excessively rare – so rare that one is forced to conclude that the dead were disposed of in a way that has left no archaeological trace. One possibility is that bodies were disposed of in rivers, either consigned to the waters to float away on rafts or cremated at the waterside, the ashes being strewn over the flow. Such a system could go some way to explaining the weapons dredged

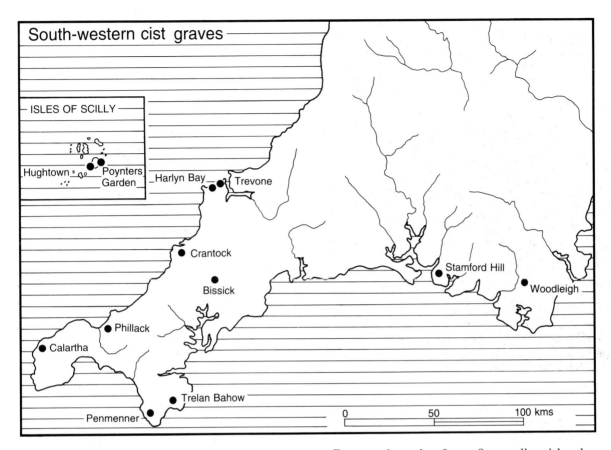

83 *Distribution of cist grave cemeteries in south-western Britain. Cemeteries of this kind are also found in Armorica reflecting the close cultural links which existed between the two peninsulas.*

from rivers. But before we begin to envisage the Thames as a British Ganges another more likely possibility should be explored – that excarnation was widespread in Iron Age Britain (**84**). Excarnation involves the exposure of the body in a tree or on a specially constructed platform and was, and indeed still is, practised in many parts of the world. In some recently observed cases it was believed that after the person had died the spirit hovered around the body for some while before finally departing. During this liminal period the body was left untouched but afterwards the bones could be treated as relics and, if necessary, could be brought back to the settlement site to be used in other parts of the belief system.

Excarnation, in fact, fits well with the archaeological evidence. It was certainly practised during the Neolithic period and there are some suggestions that after cremation had become widespread during the Bronze Age bodies may first have been exposed before the remains were consumed on the funeral pyre. The disappearance of cremation cemeteries in the seventh century may simply mean that the exposed remains were no longer cremated. To prove excarnation archaeologically is difficult but there is ample evidence from settlement sites to show that human remains were in circulation. In most cases it is isolated bones that are found mixed up with other debris but on a few occasions the discoveries suggest more deliberate deposition. At Danebury where this phenomenon has been studied in detail there is clear evidence of the deposition of parts of human bodies, still articulated, in contexts similar to those of the other special burials in

84 *Excarnation was probably the normal disposal rite for the dead over much of central southern Britain during the Iron Age. Bodies are likely to have been exposed on platforms until the flesh had largely rotted. The bones of ancestors could then be collected and used in other rituals.*

pits. It could, of course, be that these remains are those of dismembered sacrificial victims but a more likely explanation is that they were relics of ancestors brought back from the excarnation ground to be used as propitiatory offerings in the fertility ritual we have outlined above. If so, then the use of such valuable gifts could imply that society was making a particularly strong plea for divine intervention.

The reintroduction of cremation in the south-east of Britain in the first century BC need not imply that excarnation was no longer practised since, as in the earlier period, cremation could follow excarnation. Some evidence that this was so was provided by the rich burial found at Folly Lane, Verulamium. Here the noble-man was laid out in his mortuary chamber, surrounded by his grave goods for some unde-fined period, before the body was finally burnt and buried in a pit nearby.

Viewing the burial evidence overall we are left with the distinct impression that central southern Britain adhered to long-established burial traditions that were very different from those widely practised on the Continent. But in the western zone the stone-lined graves were in the same tradition as those found in Brittany, while the Arras burials of southern Yorkshire mirror closely Continental types and there is growing evidence that in Kent, too, a cemetery rite like that of adjacent Gaul may have been in operation. The picture is once more the old east/west divide, the two faces looking towards the Continent with the central south developing in its own original way.

The picture we have been able to create of the belief systems of Iron Age Britain, based largely on the archaeological evidence but enlivened with Caesar's anecdotes of contem-porary Gaulish society, gives a flavour of the complexity of the subject. The gods were every-where and ritual behaviour all-pervasive. The tribal gods had to be placated with gifts of weapons taken in battle, while the fertility deities of the earth, so vital to daily well-being of society, were revered and cajoled in seasonal acts of propitiation closely linked to the all-important reproductive cycle of the agrarian year. All this we can dimly discern but how much more complicated it must have been, so dangerously complex that ordinary men needed the close guidance of a religious elite to enable them properly to communicate with the gods and to observe the niceties of the religious calendar. Ever present would have been the knowledge that failure meant retribution.

Reading today the poet Lucan's description of a native forest sanctuary near Massilia destroyed by Caesar we can begin to grasp something of the fear of it all:

> gods were worshipped there with savage rites, the altars heaped with hideous offerings and every tree sprinkled with human blood. On those boughs...birds feared to perch, in those coverts wild beasts would not lie down; no wind ever bore down upon that wood...the trees, even when they spread their leaves to no breeze rustled of them-selves....The images of the gods, grim and rude were uncouth blocks formed of felled tree-trunks – their mere antiquity and the ghastly hue of their rotten timber struck terror....

9

The Iron Age achievement: a longer perspective

It is no exaggeration to say that the Iron Age marked a turning point in British history. It was a period of re-formation following the end of the Neolithic-Bronze Age cycle of socio-economic development and standing at the beginnings of a new cycle, which was to last until the high medieval period when the overseas exploration once more changed the direction and quickened the pace. The scale of transformation can best be appreciated by contrasting the situation in say 1300 BC with that on the eve of the Roman conquest.

The Neolithic-Bronze Age cycle was a time when societies were developing food-producing strategies and evolving social systems to enable sedentary groups to live together in some degree of harmony. Economically progress was slow but steady. Agricultural clearances were carved out of the wild, only to revert from time to time, while the balance between cereals and animals constantly changed as crises demanded new strategies. In short, it was a time of experiments – of a juddering momentum towards a more open and more tamed landscape. Socially, however, it was a time of staggering change. Huge building projects, such as the construction of Avebury and Silbury Hill, brought disparate groups together in acts of communal endeavour. Society began to flex the muscles of coercive power. All this, it seems, in the interests of monumentalizing the concept of lineage and establishing a relationship to the deities glimpsed through lunar and solar phenomena.

To accomplish these great building works required society to produce surplus food but these projects were localized in both space and time. The continuous production of a surplus is, however, implicit in the appearance and movement of luxury items – first the fine stone axes and later copper (and its alloy bronze), gold, amber and faience. By the second millennium it seems that a social system had evolved in most parts of the country, headed by an elite able to command the movement of rare raw materials and manifesting its legitimacy in elaborate burial ritual. Throughout this long period of development it is highly probable that population increased but nowhere are there indications that the landscape was densely settled.

The period of transition, from c. 1300–800, marked the end of the old system and the beginning of the new. Land came under increasingly rigorous control with newly organized field systems and linear boundaries, and homesteads, for the first time in most areas, took on the appearance of semi-permanence. Alongside this the old religious monuments seem to have been largely abandoned. In this, surely, we are witnessing a major shift away from a lunar/solar-dominated religion to beliefs more closely related to ensuring the fertility of the soil. It may be that it was in this period that the cycle of agrarian festivals became firmly established – festivals which, in different guises, are still a part of our calendar today.

Certainly, by the sixth century grain storage had become a significant aspect of settlement sites, and complex rites, involving the pit storage of seed corn accompanied by propitiation, were underway in the central southern region.

These new aspects of religious beliefs developed alongside traditional systems which required that weapons, dedicated to the deities, were thrown into lakes and rivers. The dead seem, in many regions, now to have been removed from the realms of the earth altogether and kept in the sphere of the sky (that is placed on excarnation platforms), though the use of parts of bodies as propitiatory offerings in pits shows that rigorous divides were not maintained.

What initiated these transformations is difficult to say. Undoubtedly the simplest explanation would be to assume that pressure on resources brought about in large measure by a steady increase in population, and exacerbated in some areas by climatic deterioration, was the prime mover. Such pressures would explain the need to take firmer control of the land and to focus on more efficient production of food. What had been a **sufficer economy**, producing only what was sufficient to maintain the group and to support its social acts, began to turn towards becoming a **maximizer economy**, in which the land was made to be productive and agrarian surpluses were needed to support more people occupying the same land. These may have been some of the pressures which society was experiencing at the beginning of the Iron Age.

Over the seven centuries or so of the Iron Age, life in Britain had changed out of all recognition. Two trends in particular stand out. The first is the density and permanence of the settlement pattern. New settlements were being created throughout the country and the majority, once established, continued in use. By the first century BC, over great tracts of Britain, it would have been impossible to have looked out across a landscape without seeing dozens of farmsteads. This phenomenon was specifically remarked upon by Julius Caesar. What this means in terms of actual population is difficult to say. In one area of the South Downs, in the parish of Chalton, a detailed survey implies that the population in the second century BC was at least equivalent to that in the seventeenth century AD. It would be wrong to extrapolate figures too widely but suggestions that the population of Britain may have reached 4–5 million by the time of the Roman invasion may not be too wide of the mark. If so then the Iron Age must have experienced a population growth of near exponential proportions equivalent to that of some developing countries today – indeed the analogy may be highly appropriate.

The second dominating trend is one of intensification of production. Quite simply the quantity and variety of artefacts in circulation by the last years of the pre-Roman era had increased phenomenally compared with the beginning of the period seven centuries earlier, and this is true even if the comparison is made with the period before the contact with the Roman world had begun c. 100 BC. The implication must be that an increasing part of society's energy was being devoted to the extraction of raw materials and to manufacture. The corollary is that systems of exchange must have become more complex. Such a development could be expected to follow an increase in population.

This intensification is a far more complex issue than simply the greater availability of more commodities: it takes with it the implication of technological advance. This is seen at a basic level in crop growing. More types of crop come into production, with winter-sown varieties becoming more frequent, allowing a more efficient use of the varied micro-environments now being colonized. In parallel with this the wooden ox-drawn ard began to be tipped with iron to create a more durable implement (**85**). Nor should we forget the development of vehicle construction. The carts found in the Arras burials of the fourth century

85 *An Iron Age plough team at work. The 'plough' is more strictly termed an ard which simply scored the ground and did not turn the sod. If the fields had been first 'rooted over' by pigs the 'ploughing' would have been much easier.*

BC were finely crafted with elaborate spoked wheels, with iron 'tires' shrunk on, and these techniques were evidently taken to a high degree of technical perfection in the specialized war chariot of the first centuries BC and AD. Indeed carriage building, in all its essentials,

was a fully developed craft in Britain by the time of the Roman invasion. Absence of firm evidence prevents us from tracing its origins but in all probability the technology was introduced from the Continent in the sixth or fifth century at the earliest.

Another very considerable advance was that of rotary motion. The rotary hand-quern – a grindstone for corn – makes its first appearance in Britain at a surprisingly early date in the fourth or third century BC – long before, it would seem, it became known in the Mediterranean

86 *Farmer using a rotary quern to grind grain. The rotary quern was introduced into Britain during the Iron Age replacing the older type of saddle quern.*

114

(**86**). Here we may be seeing a technological invention emanating from the barbarian world. Another possibility in the same category is the barrel. Although the evidence for this is far less tangible, the inhabitants of southern Gaul at the time of the Roman contact were renowned for their skills as coopers and it may well have been from this region that the Romans eventually learned the advantages of the barrel over the more fragile and cumbersome wine amphorae.

Knowledge of ironworking was probably introduced into the British Isles quite early. From a lake at Llyn Fawr, in south Wales, amid a number of items of the seventh century BC thrown there as part of a ritual deposit, came an iron sickle made in a form directly copying local bronze types. It must have been manufactured locally. How the knowledge of iron production actually reached Britain is uncertain, but one distinct possibility is that the pyrotechnic skills were introduced along the Atlantic sea-ways, the early smiths extracting their iron from the ferrocupric ores of the south-west. Other technologies introduced into Britain during the Iron Age include the manufacture of glass beads and probably bracelets, the use of the lathe for turning bracelets and vessels from shale, and the potter's wheel (**87, 88, 89**).

Intensification in production, in terms of both the quantity of goods generated and their variety is, perhaps, the most striking aspect of the economic development of the British Iron Age. An inhabitant of Wessex of the sixth century BC might have found the world of the second century BC a startling place, though still familiar, but transported to the early first century AD he would have felt totally alienated: the velocity of change was exponential.

The growth of population and the increased intensity of production were closely related phenomena, each intensifying the other. Such a system is likely to have generated a situation of social stress especially if population numbers approached too closely the holding capacity of the land and thus required a readjustment of

87 *Wheel-turned shale vessel from Chesterford, Essex. Kimmeridge shale was extracted from coastal exposures on the 'Isle' of Purbeck, Dorset. The technique of wheel-turning to make pottery and to turn shale seems to have been introduced into central southern Britain about 100 BC. Wheel-turned pots and shale vessels were very similar in form.*

consumption patterns relating to the display of elite status. As we have seen, throughout most parts of Britain in the early stages there was a tendency to create imposing settlement structures usually enclosed within boundaries of defensive proportions. This can be seen as a symbol of two types of dominance – the dominance of man over the land and the dominance of one lineage over the other.

There is no need to interpret any of this as evidence of aggression; indeed it may well be that over large tracts of the British Isles the natural aggression of the population was contained entirely within symbolic systems – at least for most of the time. There must, however, have been outbreaks of violence and in some regions, like central southern Britain, it may well have been sustained. The developed hillforts, and more particularly the complex propitiatory rites and the evidence of battle-scarred skeletons, all point to a situation of stress which may have been exacerbated by factors such as population growth and the depletion of the thin downland soils.

88 *Iron fire-dogs from Lords Bridge, Barton, Cambridgeshire. Work of this kind shows the ironsmith's mastery of his materials and his love of simple elegant forms. Pairs of fire-dogs adorned hearths which provided the focus of the social gathering.*

The bow-wave effect of the Romanization of Gaul deflected indigenous developments – at least in the south-east. It created new outlets for surplus, which must have increased the desire to produce surpluses, and by introducing a market for slaves encouraged slave raiding in peripheral regions. The overall effect of this may have led to sustained growth and stabilization in the south-east but to destabilization elsewhere. This was the situation which the Romans inherited when, in AD 43, they began their conquest.

The brief interlude of Romanization totally failed to bring about any lasting change in the British Isles. The Roman urban system was already showing signs of failure within a century of its imposition and by the fourth century AD it could be argued that native systems of social and economic organization were beginning to reassert themselves beneath the thin veneer of Romanization. The situation which developed in the fifth and sixth centuries AD, even allowing for the influx of new settlers from the Continent, was not at all unlike that of the third and second centuries BC. Only by the seventh and eighth centuries had British society begun to reach the level of development of the early first century AD. The only effect of the Roman interlude, and the Germanic incursions which followed, was to deflect and retard the natural growth of British society for more than half a millennium.

Let us now, finally, stand back from the story of the Iron Age in an attempt to see it in its longer perspective. The British Isles are, and always have been, part of two systems – a western Atlantic system and a northern Continental system, the seas, on many occasions, forming a stronger bond between the two outward-looking communities than the land between.

The Atlantic sea-ways linked the metal-rich west, with its predominantly older, harder rocks, and its wetter oceanic climate. Along these routes concepts of domestication spread and a little later societies adopted similar types of collective megalithic tombs together with their grammar of engraved art. Growth in the use of bronze as a general-purpose material intensified contact and, even though iron soon replaced it, copper, tin and the often associated silver and gold were still avidly sought. The ebb and flow of coastal and trans-peninsular traffic continued and may even have intensified. Briefly, Roman entrepreneurs benefited from these systems, which showed a willingness to carry Italian wine and native slaves. In the mêlée which followed the collapse of the Roman state little changed except that people as well as commodities moved in larger numbers. Religious leaders from Ireland and Wales passed through Cornwall to Brittany to minister to a population of Gaulish Celts enhanced by an influx of British Celts, while ships bearing

89 *A bronze fitting in the form of a bull, from Bulbury, Dorset. The animal was one of a pair and may have ornamented a yoke by means of which horses were attached to chariots or carts. The more efficient horse collar was not introduced into western Europe from the east until much later.*

imported pottery and wine from the Mediterranean reached Cornwall, the Irish Sea and the west coasts of Scotland. Later, in the thirteenth and fourteenth centuries, wine from Gascony and the Saintonge regions of western France was brought in quantity to the ports of Britain to satisfy the burgeoning urban population of Britain. The still-flourishing port-wine trade is a direct linear descendant of these systems – a reminder that the Atlantic sea-ways are still a reality.

The northern Continental system linked the agricultural lands of the newer softer rocks – a region enjoying a drier, colder climate. The contacts across the North Sea and in particular the narrower southern approaches persisted throughout prehistory, culminating, after Caesar's campaigns, in a close mesh of social and economic interactions which led to striking cultural similarities between the Aylesford-Swarling culture of Britain and the southern Belgic culture of Gaul. The narrowness of the English Channel attracted the Roman invasion forces in 55 and 54 BC and AD 43 and provided a safe link for the considerable volume of commerce as well as for troop movements. Later, in the third century, the seas became attractive to marauders from the Continental coastal lands north of the Rhine – first pirates, then confederate settlers allowed in under Roman licence and later raiders and settlers in a more uncontrolled flow. The pattern repeated some centuries later when more northern peoples – the Vikings – began to plunder and then settle the east coast regions, but such was the force of the movement that more adventurous bands penetrated and utilized the Atlantic system northwards, via the Orkneys and Shetlands and southwards to the Armorican peninsula and beyond. It was a long process which culminated in the landing of the Norman invasion force in 1066. Thereafter the North Sea provided the vehicle for sporadic raids in both directions, and for the growth of a massive volume of trade linking British ports from Aberdeen to Sandwich with their Continental neighbours from Bergen to Calais.

In their varied regional manifestations the Iron Age communities of Britain were conditioned by the unshakeable realities of geography which, over millennia, imposed a pattern of constraints and opportunities leading to similar and recurring solutions. Against this *longue durée* it was a time of massive change, spanning the transformation from the first cycle of socio-economic development of the Neolithic-Bronze Age to the system which was to operate, with little significant change, until the fifteenth century AD. What makes it even more intriguing is that it was during the Iron Age that the first-named Britons emerged into history, woad-painted, torc-wearing and clad in bright woven fabrics – real men and women whose motives and actions, though only vaguely revealed, we can begin to respond to. Britain had ceased to be anonymous.

Glossary

amphora Ceramic container used for the transport of wine and oil from the Mediterranean.

ard Simple form of plough. The ard simply breaks the soil while the plough breaks and turns the sod.

Arras Culture Name given by archaeologists to a distinctive cultural group occupying an area just north of the Humber estuary, in the fifth to first centuries BC.

broch Large, circular stone-built house sometimes of tower-like proportions. Found in northern Britain, predominately on the Western and Northern Isles and the adjacent mainland of Scotland.

co-axial Applied to field systems laid out together in a regular chequer-board pattern.

cist-graves Graves lined and capped with stone slabs.

colonia A deliberate settlement of retired Roman soldiers.

Dressel 1A and 1B Terminology used to distinguish two types of Italian amphorae (named after the archaeologist who classified them). Type 1A were in use in the second and first centuries BC; Type 1B came into use only in the middle of the first century BC.

en échelon Military term used to describe defences which are discontinuous, with one stepped out in front of another.

faience A blue glass-like substance used mainly in jewellery.

Hallstatt Archaeological terminology used to refer to the later part of the Late Bronze Age and early part of the Iron Age; roughly 1200–500 BC. Named after a cemetery site in Austria.

La Tène Terminology used for the later part of the Iron Age (fifth century BC to Roman). Named after a site in Switzerland.

lynchet Bank formed at the end of a field by soil which, loosened by the plough, gradually moves down slope by gravity and erosion.

multivallate Defences composed of more than one bank and ditch.

oppidum Imprecise term used to refer to large settlements of town-like proportions.

terret ring Ring, usually of bronze, for joining a horse harness.

Places to visit

Museums

Archaeological finds from Iron Age sites are plentiful and sometimes spectacular. The most comprehensive collections are to be found, as one might expect, in the three national museums:

The British Museum, London

The National Museum of Scotland, Edinburgh

The National Museum of Wales, Cardiff.

Many other museums have much to offer. Among those with major Iron Age holdings on display are:

The Museum of the Iron Age, Andover, Hants. (housing the finds from Danebury)

The Dorset County Museum, Dorchester, Dorset (including the Maiden Castle Collection)

The Somerset County Museum, Taunton, Somerset

The Devizes Museum, Devizes, Wilts.

Salisbury Museum, Salisbury, Wilts.

The Lewes Museum, Lewes, East Sussex

Colchester Museum, Colchester, Essex

The Ashmolean Museum, Oxford, Oxon

The Museum of Archaeology and Ethnography, Cambridge, Cambs.

The Yorkshire Museum, York

Hull Museum (for material from the Arras burials)

Northamptonshire Museum, Northampton, Northants.

The Red House Museum, Christchurch, Dorset.

Sites in England

Iron Age sites abound, the most obvious being **defended sites** like hillforts, rounds (Cornwall), raths (Wales), and the homesteads, the brochs and the duns of northern Britain. The Ordnance Survey maps (1:50,000 scale) mark the more obvious while the Ordnance Survey *Map of Southern Britain in the Iron Age* provides an incomparable vision of the Iron Age landscape, though on a much smaller scale. The best available guidebook is James Dyer, *Southern England: an Archaeological Guide* (Faber).

To select sites for special mention from so vast an array is an invidious task but among the most representative of the hillforts of England in public ownership or easy of access we should mention:

Blackbury Castle, Devon

Worlbury, Somerset

Maiden Castle, Dorset

Hengistbury Head, Dorset

Bratton Camp, Wilts.

Danebury, Hants.

Old Winchester Hill, East Meon, Hants.

Beacon Hill, Hants.

Uffington Castle and the White Horse, Oxon

Old Oswestry, Salop

Herefordshire Beacon, Hereford & Worcs.
Midsummer Hill, Hereford & Worcs.
Almondbury, Huddersfield, W. Yorks.
Ingleborough, W. Yorks.
Other major defensive earthworks belonging to oppida may be seen at:

Chichester Entrenchments, W. Sussex
Lexden, Colchester, Essex
Stanwick, Yorks.

Settlement sites are much rarer but three may be visited in Cornwall at:

Carn Euny
Chysauster
Halliggye Fogou (an underground storage chamber).

Visible settlement remains exist elsewhere, e.g. in the Pennines, the Cheviots, on Exmoor, Dartmoor and Bodmin, and the Peak District, but these are often on private land.

Sites in Wales

For sites in Wales the would-be visitor is advised to consult the excellent series of regional guides:

A Guide to Ancient and Historic Wales. Four volumes published by Cadw.

Glamorgan and Gwent Elizabeth Whittle
Dyfed Sian Rees
Gwynedd (forthcoming)
Clwyd and Powys (forthcoming).

Among the more dramatic sites deserving a visit we may list the following hillforts and cliff castles:

Foel Trigarn, Crymmych, Dyfed
Castell Henllys, Newport, Dyfed
Caerau promontory forts, St David's, Dyfed
St David's Head, St David's, Dyfed
Dale and Great Castle Head Forts, Dale, Dyfed
Bosherston promotory fort, Dyfed
Pen Dinas, Aberystwyth, Dyfed
Caerau hillfort, Cardiff, Gwent
Nash Point Fort, Marcross, Gwent
Tredegar Hillfort, Newport, Gwent
Llanmelin Wood Hillforts, Caerwent, Gwent

Penycloddiau hillfort, Clwyd
Moel y Gaer, Rhosemor, Clwyd
Pen y Corddyn, Abergele, Clwyd
Tre'r Ceiri, Gwynedd
Garn Boduan, Gwynedd
Carn Fadrun, Gwynedd.

Sites in Scotland

For Scotland consult

Exploring Scotland's Heritage. Eight volumes published by the Royal Commission on the Ancient and Historical Monuments of Scotland.

Argyle and the Western Isles Graham Ritchie and Mary Harman
Dumfries and Galloway Geoffrey Stell
Lothian and the Borders John R. Baldwin
The Highlands Joanna Close-Brooks
The Clyde Estuary and Central Region J.B. Stevenson
Orkney and Shetland Anna Ritchie
Grampian Ian Shepherd
Fife and Tayside Bruce Walker and Graham Ritchie.

There are so many Iron Age monuments to visit in Scotland that selecting a few to list here is even more difficult than for Wales and England but the highlights that should not be missed include:

Dun Ardtreck Broch, Skye
Dun Mor Broch, Vaul, Tiree
Dun Nosebridge, Islay
Broch of Guerness, Orkney
Midhowe Broch, Rousay, Orkney
Clickhimin, Lerwick, Shetland
Broch of Mousa, Shetland
Ness of Burgi, Shetland
Dun Telve Broch, Glenelg, Lochalsh
Dun Troddan Broch, Glenelg, Lochalsh
Kilphedir broch and hut circles, Sutherland
Eildon Hill North, Ettrick
The Chesters fort, East Lothian
Tealing souterrain, Dundee District.

Further reading

General books on the Celts

The Celts Sabatino Moscati (ed.) (Milan 1991)

The Celtic World Barry Cunliffe (London 1979)

The Celts T.G.E. Powell (London 1958)

The Druids Stuart Piggott (London 1968)

The Gods of the Celts Miranda Green (Gloucester 1986)

Celtic Art Ruth and Vincent Megaw (London 1989)

Iron Age Britain: General works

Iron Age Communities in Britain Barry Cunliffe (London: 3rd edn 1991)

Celtic Art Ian Stead (London 1985)

The Celtic Coinage of Britain R.D. Van Arsdell (London 1989)

Prehistoric Houses in Britain Malcolm L. Reid (Aylesbury 1993)

Regional studies

Brochs of Scotland J.N.G. Ritchie (Aylesbury 1988)

Beyond the Brochs Ian Armit (ed.) (Edinburgh 1990)

Aspects of the Iron Age in Central Southern Britain Barry Cunliffe and David Miles (eds.) (Oxford 1984)

The Arras Culture Ian Stead (York 1979)

Individual sites

By South Cadbury is that Camelot Leslie Alcock (London 1972)

Maiden Castle Niall M. Sharples (London 1991)

Danebury Barry Cunliffe (London: 2nd edn 1993)

Hengistbury Head Barry Cunliffe (London 1978)

Index